HUNTER DERBY

Also by Kim Ablon Whitney

The Perfect Distance
Blue Ribbons
Summer Circuit
Winter Circuit

Hunter
DERBY

Kim Ablon Whitney

ISBN 9781539980865

Cover by Littera Designs
Cover photos by Sassy Strides Photography and Fotolia
Text set in Sabon

Chapter 1

IF A HORSE WENT in one spot in a stall, it was easy to clean. But it also stunk to the high heavens. Zoe liked most horse smells but the acrid stench of urine was not one of them. The dark pee-soaked shavings weighed a ton as she pitched them into the wheelbarrow that jutted halfway into the stall.

Beyond the smell, there was the absolute indignity of the fact that she was here, in this small, backyard barn, mucking stalls. Okay, at first she had been thrilled to avoid any consequences larger than probation and community service.

It had been undeserved, like when someone gets you a gift that's much too generous and you don't know what to say or how to thank them. People she rode horses for as a junior used to do that. Since they couldn't pay her, they gave her expensive gifts like a new riding coat, a beautiful cashmere sweater, or once a gorgeous Hermes belt with the H for the buckle.

Now, though, she hadn't ridden a horse for anyone besides Linda Maro in weeks and she was stuck spending her mornings at Narrow Lane, a therapeutic riding center, cleaning stalls.

But the fact that she'd gotten off with community service as her only punishment was a true gift. After helping Étienne steal thousands of dollars in saddles—even though she hadn't seen any of the money, it all went to him—she could have easily found herself starring in *Orange Is The New Black*.

When she had gotten her assignment to Narrow Lane, she had assumed she'd be leading mentally or physically disabled people around, but it turned out that she apparently wasn't even good enough to shuffle around a ring dragging a half-dead horse. Instead, she had to muck out the stalls of a motley crew of horses that in no way even came close to resembling the athletic animals she usually spent time around.

She swore these horses' piss smelled worse than that of horses on the circuit.

There was Daisy, a ridiculously feminine name for what was actually a squat so-ugly-it's-cute, Fjord. Danny, a black Quarter Horse. And Pepper, a leopard Appaloosa, perhaps the ugliest kind of Appaloosa there was, which was kind of like discussing the grossest kind of throw-up. Appaloosas were all gross to Zoe; it was just a matter of degrees. Sure every now and then an Appy somehow managed to win on the A circuit. It always made the headlines of *The Chronicle* because of its sheer improbability.

As Zoe lifted the plastic pitchfork, all that ran through her head was, *Zoe Tramell is cleaning a crappy Appy's stall.* She didn't usually talk or think about herself in the third person but somehow whenever she was at Narrow Lane, that kind of thinking took over her brain. There was a lot of time to think because she was left alone to muck all the stalls, sweep, and make up the grain.

The second day she'd put in her ear buds, content to lose herself in Country music, but Kirsten, the director, informed her that she couldn't just "space out." That this wasn't a regular barn and they might need to get her attention. And for that matter Kirsten had to put in that wearing ear buds in any barn wasn't a good idea because you wouldn't hear things happening around you and you might miss a loose horse or another person calling for help. Like that stopped anyone on the show circuit from mucking with music pumping in their ears. Or riding with ear buds in for that matter.

Zoe filled the wheelbarrow and maneuvered it out to the manure pile. Before she dumped it and the flies that were hovering on the turds flew up into her face, she stopped and wiped the sweat from her forehead. At least doing the stalls would help keep her skinny since she wasn't riding more than two or three horses a day and the meds she was now taking had definitely added five or ten pounds.

She'd needed to gain weight after how scary skinny she'd become on a diet of coffee and pills. But she didn't want to get fat—fat was a death sentence to hunter riders. She'd rather lose an arm than blow up like Denise Moralle, whom everyone snickered about behind her back. She was coming to see, after just a few weeks, how the meds were helping her, even if they did have some side effects. She sometimes laughed to herself about how she'd traded illegal drugs for legal ones.

It was the counselor she saw in Wellington for her court-ordered outpatient treatment that brought up the possibility that Zoe might be bipolar. Sure, Zoe had heard of the condition but it had never occurred to her that her problems could be due to anything besides her own sheer stupidity and shitty upbringing.

The counselor had taken her history and asked thorough questions about Zoe's moods and emotions. She nodded along as Zoe recounted years of highs and lows, crazy nights out when she couldn't sleep, followed by days when she slugged through life, feeling miserable.

"So am I bipolar?" Zoe had asked.

The counselor said yes, she thought so. Zoe expected to feel terrible about having such a weighty diagnosis thrust on her but if anything, she felt relief. *This explains so much*, she thought. The counselor's description of the symptoms of bipolar was like someone exactly describing her life and feelings. Zoe thought, *How did you know what it feels like to be me?*

It wasn't just that she was fucked up anymore—she had a reason for being so fucked up. Not an excuse. But a reason. And best of all, the counselor thought with medication, Zoe's life might get a lot easier. It wasn't like the medication would solve everything. Zoe still had to make better choices but it would even out her intense, roller coaster moods.

Pepper was the last stall of the morning. She put in new shavings and pulled the banks down. They didn't have three-foot banks here like they did at show barns. Tiny swirls of shaving dust danced in the sunlight slanting into the barn. All that was left was sweeping the aisle, thank the Lord. She grabbed a broom, wishing they used a leaf-blower like most normal people. But they probably believed that it wasn't good because all the shavings and dust went up to the ceiling and into the horses' lungs.

With the aisle now clean, she said a quick goodbye to Kirsten and headed to her car. One good thing about coming early was she had yet to see an actual lesson. Usually when she was pulling out, the first modified-minivan of the day would be pulling in and a tired-looking parent would be getting out and letting down the motorized ramp. Today was no exception and Zoe sped out before she saw who would be coming down that ramp.

She braked at the end of the driveway as a horse and rider across the street caught her eye. She'd noticed there was a horse farm there before but assumed it was some backyard place like Narrow Lane. Or at least not a fancy show barn.

But the horse and rider looked legit. A bay warmblood with an impressive trot. A man who knew how to ride. It was amazing how in a split second a good rider could tell if another horse and rider were 'A' Circuit material, or not.

She couldn't tell how old he was exactly but he looked to be in her general range for guys—somewhere between twenty and forty-five. But if he was anybody, she would have known he was here in Bedford, New York. She knew everyone who was anyone.

Which meant he was a nobody.

Of course, he could be a step down from the professionals she was used to but not a total nobody. Maybe he showed locally and didn't go to WEF or win at Indoors. It was possible. Unlikely, but possible.

She felt a small dash of hope flutter somewhere inside her. Could something good come out of this terrible assignment at Narrow Lane? Her mind raced to preposterous fantasies. Not so much about falling in love with him, but about his having really nice horses and wanting her to ride and show them. She would pop up at Old Salem and everyone would be in total disbelief that she'd put her life back together, found a great job, and was back in the show ring. She'd win every class that mattered in the professional divisions.

Zoe nearly shivered thinking about herself winning again. She envisioned landing off the last jump after she'd nailed a course and all the ensuing clapping and whooping. She heard the announcer's excited voice saying she'd scored a 94 and a 96 in the handy round of the hunter derby. All of a sudden, it would be like she was a top junior again.

Of course that was her fantasy. Her reality was that her shoulders hurt from cleaning all the stalls, she had shaving dust up her nose, and now it was time to hustle over to Linda's to ride a few of Dakota's horses.

Chapter 2

WALKING INTO Morada Bay East was like walking into a real house after going camping. Well, Zoe had never actually been camping but that's what she assumed it was like. Or maybe it was like staying in a hotel room on the road after living in a small camper at the showgrounds.

For a few months when she was sixteen, Zoe had dated a grand prix rider who lived in a camper, and it wasn't a nice camper either. Spending nights in a box where you could practically touch both walls had gotten old fast. Maybe that was why the relationship hadn't lasted. Although there were other reasons too, including that she'd cheated on him. He was still around but had never made it big. Mostly competed in smaller grand prix classes and had a decent sales and training business.

Morada Bay was simply gorgeous. The barn was only a few years old, built by one of the premier equestrian architecture firms. An old barn on the property had been restored and turned into a quaint vehicle and equipment storage area. The new 12-stall barn was sunny and well lit, with beautiful exposed cherry beams. The aisles were lined with interlocking rubber pavers so no horse would ever slip or fall.

The grass surrounding the barn was Pixar-green from underground sprinklers and a flock of guinea hens scuttled around, pecking the ground. They were part decoration for their polka-dot feathers, part organic pest removal for their penchant for devouring large quantities of ticks, mosquitoes, and other unwanted bugs.

"Hey, there," Linda said as Zoe came into the barn.

Just being at an 'A' class facility lifted her spirits immeasurably. A few horses hung their heads over the stall doors. Each one was muscled and handsome, with well-trimmed manes. Others were turned out in their fly sheets and masks in the well-kept pastures.

"Hi-ya." Zoe headed toward the whiteboard to see whom she was riding today. It varied from day to day. She saw she was down for Logan, Midway, and Plato. Dakota would be coming out after school to ride a few of the others. Linda had hurt her back packing up the barn after WEF and was grounded for a while, which was why Zoe was riding for them. The job had come up at just the right time, with Hannah's help, of course.

When news spread that Zoe had been involved with the rash of saddle thefts at WEF and was taking all kinds of pills, no one was exactly racing to hire her. Most people on the circuit had known about the drugs, but no one had known about her helping Étienne steal thousands of dollars in saddles by helping him get access to locked tack rooms.

Other people did pretty awful things in the show world and later resuscitated their careers. Zoe hoped she could do the same, but in the meantime she needed to keep clean and have a job that paid her enough to live. Riding for Dakota served that purpose.

"I have you down for three," Linda said, coming to stand beside her.

"Great," Zoe said. "How's the back?"

Linda gritted her teeth. "Still sucks."

Zoe liked Linda a lot. Every so often you met a normal, non-judgmental, down-to-earth horse person and Linda was one of those people. Linda had welcomed Zoe to Morada Bay at a time when most people were turning their backs on her. She never seemed suspicious or wary of her, like maybe she needed extra supervision. She gave her the codes to the tack trunks right away and had even asked her to go into the main house several times. Linda really trusted her, despite her past history.

Dakota's parents had hired a famous interior designer to decorate the main house but they were never there. Both were renowned heart surgeons and most of the year were out of the country on humanitarian missions. On the rare occasion they were in the U.S., usually to accept some award at a charity gala, they stayed in their New York City brownstone.

As much as Zoe liked Linda and didn't want her to be in pain, if Linda's back improved and she could ride again, Zoe would be out of a job. Maybe by then she'd be done with her community service and would have found a job riding and showing again for a big barn.

But for now, the few hundred dollars she made just barely paid the rent on her shitty furnished studio apartment, her gas, and her meals. Plus, riding at Morada Bay was the only thing that still connected her to the show circuit.

"I saw this guy riding today at the farm across from Narrow Lane," Zoe said to Linda.

"John Bradstreet."

"I guess." Zoe felt a wave of disappointment at not even vaguely recognizing the name. "Who is he?"

"Has a small sales business. Importing horses and making them up. He takes them to some of the shows around here."

"Hunters or jumpers?"

"A little bit of both. He rides well but he's never really done anything big, you know? He rode around here as a junior."

The automatic fly spray system went on overhead, releasing a fine mist of organic repellent.

"I'm surprised I've never heard of him," Zoe said.

Linda gave a moderated shrug—a result of her injury. She also sported a back brace. "Kind of keeps a low profile."

Zoe turned from the whiteboard. "Gay?" It was the next obligatory question when talking about a rider with XY chromosomes.

"No."

"With someone?"

"No, single, as far as I know. Kinda cute too."

Usually Zoe would have been excited that he was cute but right now she cared more about what his horses were like.

"Nice guy," Linda continued. "Too young for me. He's probably about your age . . . maybe a few years older."

"What do you need a guy for?" Zoe said. "You've got Eamon."

Right before she had injured her back, actually the night Hannah had gone crazy and messed around with McNair Sutter, torching her relationship with Chris Kern possibly forever, Linda had hooked up with an Irish guy. Eamon was one of the nice ones. A one-night stand between Linda and Eamon had surprisingly turned into a relationship. Eamon worked for a grand prix rider in New Jersey, and so far things between him and Linda were going well.

"I know, I keep forgetting I'm actually in a functioning relationship." Linda gave a wry shake of her head. "It's nearly amazing."

"You deserve it," Zoe said.

Linda smiled. "I know. I actually do. After all the losers I dated over the years, I deserve to date the nice guy."

"Don't even talk to me about dating losers," Zoe said. "My list is long and I'm younger than you."

"If it can happen for me, it can happen for you," Linda said.

"I don't even care about guys right now. I just need to put my head down and get my life back on track."

"You'll get there," Linda said. "I know you will."

Linda went into the office to place orders for grain and schedule the farrier and Zoe got on her first horse. She knew Hannah loved Midway—that second to Logan he had been her favorite and she could see why. He was the horse equivalent of that nice guy Zoe should be dating and Linda was.

Midway framed up naturally. He went in a simple loose ring and Zoe always had a perfect light connection between her hands and his mouth. He never pulled or lugged. He was supple in both directions and responsive to her leg. He was so easy that the problem was Zoe would ride him for ten minutes and then feel like there was nothing left to do.

With a harder horse, Zoe would get lost in trying to fix a shoulder that was popping out or a stiff side, and the time would fly by. Forty minutes later, she'd finally come to a walk, both she and the horse huffing but having accomplished some improvement. There was nothing to improve on Midway. But he needed to stay fit so to keep things from getting boring she counter-cantered him in both directions and cantered over rails on the ground.

After she was done with Midway, she traded him to a groom for Logan. Logan wasn't as easy as Midway but he was a hundred million times better than he used to be. It was really a miracle how far he'd come from the horse he'd been when Hannah had first gotten him. He still needed a reminder to listen to her aids so Zoe spent her time lengthening and shortening his stride. When she got off, she snapped a picture of Logan and snapchatted it to Hannah. He was reaching out to touch her phone with his nose so it was a pretty funny shot.

When you miss your first mom, she wrote.

Dakota arrived at the barn, ferried by her newest nanny, Angelique. Zoe rode her last horse at the same time as Dakota rode Dudley. Dakota seemed to have sprouted up a few inches since Florida, if that was even possible. It was hard to believe that not that long ago she'd been riding ponies. Now, she was fully a junior rider. Whereas at first she'd looked slightly small on Dudley, she fit all 16.2 hands of him perfectly now. If she grew much more, she might have to get a bigger eq horse. Her blonde hair was in a thick braid down her back, sticking out of her Samshield helmet.

It was fun to have someone else in the ring. When they were both done flatting, Zoe came to walk next to her so they could chit-chat. As she asked Dakota about school and life, Zoe's phone buzzed. It was a reply coming in from Hannah.

Was in class, Hannah wrote back. *I miss that sweet boy too.*

Dakota's here, Zoe replied with one hand and the other on the buckle of the reins.

Tell her I say hi.

"Hannah says hi," Zoe said.

"Tell her to come back to work for us," Dakota said. Then she shook her head. "No, don't say that. I don't want her to feel bad. She should be at school, don't you think?"

Zoe stuck her phone back in her pocket. "Yeah, she should. It's what she needs to do."

Zoe liked thinking of Hannah at school. Even though Zoe missed her, it was nice to know that other people had to do things they didn't exactly want to do. Hannah wanted to be with Chris but for right now that wasn't possible. She needed to be a normal college girl and figure out her life without him. She and Zoe had talked about how they both could use a break from guys.

Zoe definitely needed a break from guys—she'd been involved on some level pretty much straight since she was fourteen. The last guy she'd slept with was Morgan Cleary and that was a few weeks ago, which was pretty epic in terms of a hiatus for her. But she wondered if what Hannah actually needed was to be with *other* guys, not to take a break from guys completely. Chris had been her first boyfriend, her first time.

"Do you think she and Chris will ever get back together?" Dakota asked.

"I don't know. But if they ever do, I don't think it'll be for a while. She hurt him pretty badly."

"I liked them together," Dakota said.

"Me too."

They headed out the gate of the ring and back to the barn. Two grooms stood ready. One to take Dudley and the other had Sonny ready for Dakota. It was unspoken that Zoe would put Plato in his stall herself.

Linda shuffled out of the barn, looking nearly geriatric. She pulled her sunglasses off her head down onto her face. "Can you come back into the ring after you get him put away?" she asked Zoe. "I can't really move the jumps."

"I'll be your jump crew," Zoe said happily. She'd do anything to pitch in at Morada Bay. Zoe had taken to hanging around on the days that she didn't have to call her counselor. She was a horse person through and through—the place she felt most comfortable was the barn. She loved the way she felt at Morada Bay, the person she was there, and would stay as long each day as Linda wanted.

Chapter 3

THE NEXT MORNING after Zoe's stalls were done, Kirsten asked her to ride Pepper.

"Me?" Zoe said, although there was no one else around and it was clear that Kirsten was talking to her. "You want me to get on him?"

"Yes, that's what I said." Kirsten scratched the side of her head. She wore her hair in a French braid, and had on baggy cargo shorts and hiking boots. She didn't look like the horse people Zoe was used to. "You don't have a problem with that, do you?"

There had been no actual job description that came along with her agreement to volunteer at Narrow Lane. Maybe riding was an improvement over doing stalls but it didn't quite feel like it given the quality of the horses.

"No, I guess not," Zoe said. What choice did she have? She felt like she understood slightly better what it might be like for inmates forced to make license plates or what have you.

Kirsten pointed to the tack room. "His tack is labeled."

Each horse had a labeled bridle, saddle, and clean saddle pad. Zoe had to give them points for organization. She grabbed the bridle marked *Pepper* off the hook and went to find the saddle. She saw it and shuddered.

Bucket seat, huge pommel, long dressage-like flaps. Was it even leather?

It didn't look anything close to the six-thousand-dollar custom calfskin leather of the saddles she was used to. Maybe it was plastic or pleather. She looked closer to see the brand inscribed on the little grommet—Wintec.

She found Kirsten back in the barn. "Um, can I use my saddle? I have it in my car."

"No, the horses have to go in the saddles they're ridden in for lessons," Kirsten said curtly, leaving no room for negotiation.

Zoe slunk back into the tack room and heaved the heavy Wintec monstrosity off the rack. Using this saddle was like an NBA player forced to wear a pair of Payless sneakers for tip-off.

She brought Pepper in from the paddock and put him on the cross-ties. Of course he was caked in dirt, clumps of it matting his coat, and Narrow Lane didn't have a vacuum. Zoe did her best, currying and brushing, sending clouds of dust into the air and up her nostrils. By the time she was done, she was coated in a layer of grime. Pepper looked only marginally better. The only thing that could actually get him clean was a bath. Even a vacuum's power would have had its limits.

She put on the tack, including the saddle. It took extra

might to hoist it onto his back and the long flap hit her in the eye. She couldn't believe she was going to actually put her ass into that thing.

She led the Crappy Appy by the rubber rainbow reins into the indoor. There was no outdoor ring at Narrow Lane. Zoe assumed it was easier for the kids to hang on inside without rustling leaves or birds in the trees spooking the horses.

The only mounting block was the wheelchair ramp. Zoe led Pepper up to it and hopped on. It was amazing what a bad saddle and school-horse-type could do. Just like that she no longer felt like Zoe Tramell, former star junior rider. She felt like a backyard rider who could barely post.

Kirsten appeared. Zoe thought she saw her trying to disguise a small smile. Maybe the horse didn't even need to be ridden; Kirsten just wanted to see Zoe suffer. Zoe let the stirrups down a few holes, which was a chore since the leathers were stiff. She squeezed Pepper into a walk and headed out to the rail.

"What do you want me to do with him?" she called to Kirsten.

"Just make him go forward and listen to your aids. Lots of transitions. Sometimes he can be a bit of a bully and I like to remind him who's boss."

"Do you usually ride him?" She was trying to feel out why she had been granted this opportunity.

"Sometimes," Kirsten said cryptically.

Zoe had to post enormously high to even get her butt out of the bucket seat of the saddle. Pepper's stride was short and choppy. After the horses she had spent her whole life riding, he felt like a donkey. Of course he was stiff and didn't even know what a frame was.

She tried to ignore how awful the whole thing felt and just go about her business. She rode transitions and pushed him forward and kept him straight. At the canter, she felt like she had fallen into a couch—only it was an extremely uncomfortable couch. She tried getting up in half-seat but the pommel kept ramming her in the crotch.

Pepper's canter was barely a canter; it felt like he was trotting behind but maybe that was a net positive for his job. After a while, it didn't exactly feel good but it felt better. Zoe got used to having no frame and no suppleness and she actually took a little slice of pleasure in getting Pepper to respond to her aids and demonstrate crisp transitions. Kirsten watched for a while, told her to concentrate on the walk and trot, disappeared again, then returned and told Zoe to take Pepper out on the Sensory Trail.

Zoe swiveled her head to look at her. "The what now?"

"The sensory trail. It's outside next to the driveway. It's marked—you'll see it. Just take her through it once or twice."

Kirsten opened the sliding door and Zoe rode Pepper out into the bright sunshine. Zoe sat back in the couch of a saddle, feeling like she was riding Western on a trail ride. She found the sign. *Narrow Lane Sensory Trail, donated by the Miller Family Foundation.*

It was a wide, groomed path through some trees with various stops along the way for activities, kind of like one of those exercise trails with stations to do pull-ups or sit-ups. Only instead there was a basketball hoop to throw a ball into, a mailbox to open, fake owls perched on trees that Zoe couldn't figure out what the hell they were there for, and a tree house with laminated photographs of all the horses in the barn. That one stumped her too. She stood for a few moments and looked at the hodge-podge of breeds and sizes.

Zoe wondered what horses like Pepper thought of their jobs. Did they mind carting around these kids? Most of the horses had probably been donated. This was a second chance for them. Maybe Zoe had more in common with horses like Pepper than she wanted to think about. They were all on the second stage of their career, just trying to fit in and make it work. She leaned down and begrudgingly gave the Appy a pat.

She knew some hunters and jumpers that hadn't made it for whatever reason and their owners had donated them, taking the tax-break as a kind of consolation prize and trying not to cry over the tens of thousands they'd spent going straight down the shitter. But most of those horses were donated to colleges for their riding programs. It took a special kind of attitude to be a therapeutic horse. Pepper might be the worst horse she had ever ridden but in this world he was probably one of a kind.

She looked down at his ugly spotted head. He flicked an ear back, like maybe he was communicating with her in some way.

"Come on, you old nag," she said to him rather fondly as she turned him back to the barn.

A truck was coming down the driveway. She didn't think a family would have a pick-up truck. It looked more like it might belong to a farrier or vet. But then the truck slowed to a stop next to Zoe and the window rolled down.

"You're getting to ride Pepper."

At the man's voice, Zoe turned. He was wearing breeches and boots. John Bradstreet. Even though she'd only seen him across the road, she just knew it was him. Linda was right. He was kind of cute. Black hair, fair skin, those nearly freckled lips that people with fair skin tend to have.

"Yup, I'm having the ride of my life on this Crappy Appy."

She thought it would be funny. She thought it would be something they could bond over. Laugh about. She wasn't sure why John was coming to Narrow Lane but it had to be something like to give them errant mail that had come to his address by mistake. Yet, he knew Pepper by name. They were his neighbors after all. Still, even if he was friendly with Kirsten, didn't he have to acknowledge how crappy their horses were compared to his?

But John recoiled. Whereas he'd been leaning toward Zoe, almost into the passenger seat while still keeping a hand on the wheel, now he retracted back into the truck. She most certainly wasn't winning any first impression rose with this moment.

He didn't say anything else, just drove on to the barn.

Zoe slunk back into the bucket seat of the Wintec saddle. What had she said that was so wrong?

Chapter 4

THE TEXT CAME IN while she was flopped down on the bed eating from a too large bag of Doritos. She hadn't bothered to shower yet.

Free tonight?

She sat up.

Morgan Cleary.

They had hung out a few times at the end of circuit, when she was still pretty messed up on drugs. And hung out, of course, meant slept together. Each time Zoe was interested in someone new she told herself to wait, to not sleep with him right away. But somehow it never worked.

With Morgan, she felt she had extenuating circumstances for sleeping with him. First, he was Morgan Cleary, the son of one of the wealthiest families on the circuit. Second, it was around the same time everything had come out about her and the saddle stealing and she was just so grateful that anyone, let alone someone like Morgan Cleary, would want to have anything to do with her.

After Florida, she never expected to hear from Morgan again. She was primed for a full-on ghosting and set not to let it bother her. She knew he lived in New York City and had a farm in Westchester but she didn't think he'd ever be in touch. She didn't even think he knew she was in Bedford now. But apparently he had his sources.

Think I can be. Worth canceling my other plans?

She wasn't going to tell him she was still in her riding clothes with Dorito dust all over her fingers and had absolutely no plans for the evening.

Just thinking of going to the game. Thought you might want to join.

With Morgan, just going to the game took on a different meaning. Morgan's family owned the Mets. He was currently working for a farm league affiliate, biding his time until his father let him take over as president of the big league operation. Morgan also competed in the jumpers on several very nice horses. He won nearly everything in the A/O divisions and also showed in some grand prix classes.

Zoe liked baseball well enough and she liked what being with Morgan offered—a feeling of still being relevant in the show world and a taste of the high life. If she was good enough for Morgan Cleary, wasn't she good enough for the rest of the horse show?

I'll cancel.

In her mind, baseball game equaled tiny cut-off jeans that barely reached over her butt cheeks and a gauzy off-the-shoulder shirt, paired with strappy sandals.

The fabric of her T-shirt was so thin it was nearly translucent. Her blond hair brushed against her shoulders as she checked herself out in the mirror. Perfect.

Gone was the pathetic Dorito girl. Enter pretty girl with cocky I'm-the-shit attitude.

She went to Morgan's Instagram. Most were riding shots but there were a few without his helmet. He was medium height and had brown hair. What wasn't obvious in the photos was that his hair was thinning in the back. Even in his twenties, it was pretty clear he was going bald. He was good-looking, though. Not smolderingly hot but good-looking in that way that wealthy people manage to be even if they're not blessed with gorgeous features.

She definitely didn't want Morgan seeing her depressing apartment, so she waited outside the building for him.

Morgan drove a Porsche, which wasn't a horse show car at all. Most riders drove SUVs to fit all their horse stuff and their dogs.

Zoe climbed in the passenger seat. The inside of the car was all gleaming leather. In a car like his, she could almost forget about the state of her life.

Of course any real horse person had a car that was covered in dog hair, tack, and saddle pads. But Morgan wasn't a real horse person. He could ride—that was for sure. He had talent and he won plenty of big classes. But he wasn't an in-the-trenches rider. He was the meet-the-horse-at-the-ring kind.

"You look hot," were the first words out of his mouth.

"Thank you," Zoe said, leaning back into the cool of the leather.

"What's going on?" he asked. He acted like they'd just hung out a few days ago, not like they hadn't seen each other, or even talked, in weeks.

Zoe tried to roll with it. "Not much. Rode a whole bunch today."

A whole bunch was an exaggeration. In her old life, she was used to riding eight or ten horses a day.

"Where are you working again?" Morgan said.

"For Linda Maro—Morada Bay."

She certainly wasn't going to mention anything about Narrow Lane. She assumed Morgan vaguely knew she had been in outpatient treatment and about the saddle stealing, but she wasn't going to bring it up. It must not have bothered him, or he wouldn't be taking her to the game.

"Right. Nice place," Morgan said.

"Oh, you know it?"

"We looked at it before we bought our place. It was a little too small. It's only six acres, right?"

"I don't know the exact number," Zoe said.

"It was too small," he said.

"How about you?" Zoe asked. "What did you do today?"

Morgan went on and on about his work with the team. Zoe tried to be interested. Maybe it was interesting but Morgan somehow made it seem boring. It was all about numbers and licensing deals. It had nothing to do with the players or the game.

He turned on music and it was nearly too loud to talk over, which was fine with her. He drove too fast, jockeying in and out of lanes on 95, trying to get an edge on all the other drivers but, Zoe noticed, ending up pretty much even with cars he'd passed a few miles earlier.

Intellectually she knew his driving was downright stupid but as he floored the engine and darted ahead of a car, her stomach fluttered. She gripped the sides of the seat and thought about later that night when they'd inevitably have sex. She thought of his body against hers.

They pulled up to the ballpark. As others went to great lengths to find parking or overpaid to park in a lot, Morgan turned into the owners' and players' lot. Here, his Porsche fit right in next to the Maseratis and BMWs, with the exception of the occasional pick-up truck of the redneck ballplayer that would have fit in more at a horse show than Morgan's car.

Morgan made a joke about how much parking cost for him. "100 Million and you get the best spot in the park. Such a bargain."

Everyone knew Morgan—the parking attendant, the security guards, the ticket-takers. They called him Mr. Cleary. Zoe loved how it felt to be with him. It reminded her of how she used to feel at the shows as a junior: important, belonging to the privileged class, nearly worshipped. When she used to go in the ring, it felt like the whole show stopped to watch her. She missed that feeling more than she could have ever imagined and for the moment figured she'd have to just enjoy a slice of it from being with Morgan.

Morgan was wearing khakis and a button-down shirt and next to him Zoe began to feel slightly self-conscious about her clothing choice. She had assumed they'd be passing through the main turnstiles into the ballpark like any other fan, which now—as they wound their way through the air-conditioned back office hallways of the park—she realized was completely stupid.

She had only ever been to a few ball games, most of them minor league games. One time she'd seen the Orioles at Camden Yards and another time she'd seen a game at Wrigley. Both those times she had horrible seats. She tried to shake the nagging feeling that she'd chosen the wrong clothes. Morgan hadn't said anything so maybe it didn't matter. He'd told her she looked hot.

"Julia, Bennett, and Nate are meeting us," Morgan said as they emerged onto the level of all the private boxes. Many of the boxes had gold plated signs with the names of the companies that owned them.

Zoe wasn't altogether surprised that they were meeting them. Morgan usually hung out with his pack. He'd been with them the first of the two nights he and Zoe had slept together. In a way, she was relieved it wouldn't just be her and Morgan. She wouldn't have to sit through the game alone with him, figuring out what to talk about.

They arrived at the box with the sign that read Rutherford Wallace, Inc. Morgan pushed open the door revealing a living room with leather couches, several big-screen TVs, and a full kitchen where chefs dressed in uniform stood at the ready. Zoe walked to the back of the room, which opened onto the stadium. The pitcher was warming up as the batter took practice swings on the on-deck circle.

Zoe looked out over the field, nearly transfixed. The energy in the air felt a little like before a big class.

Morgan came up behind her and put his arms around her. He nuzzled her neck and she leaned back into him. She couldn't believe how good it felt to have Morgan Cleary this into her. Why was she so lucky? Why was he even interested in her? He wasn't just asking her to his apartment so he could have sex with her. This felt like more. They were at a ball game—his friends were all coming.

"Pretty sweet," she said.

"Perks of the job," he replied.

At the sound of people entering the box, Morgan let go of her. She missed his arms around her.

Chapter 5

"HEY, MAN," Morgan called out, walking over to Nate to give him a handshake that was part high-five.

Nate was a friend of Morgan's who hung out a lot at the shows but didn't ride. He had the wrong body type for riding anyway—chubby, bordering on overweight. Zoe wasn't exactly sure how they had met but Nate was on the fringes of the wealthy, horse show posse now.

That posse also included Julia and Bennett. Julia was getting her Ph.D. at NYU in comparative biology, whatever that meant. She still had jumpers that she kept with a trainer in New Jersey but she only showed every so often.

Bennett was her best friend and showed all the time in the jumpers. She didn't have a job. "I'm taking a break after finishing college," Zoe had heard her say once.

They were both pretty and moneyed—a different class altogether than Zoe. They had gone to exclusive private schools and Ivy League colleges, they drove expensive cars, attended Fashion Week, traveled internationally, spoke other languages, and ate at the best restaurants. Their families belonged to country clubs and owned houses in multiple locations, including usually some remote tropical island.

Zoe fit in with them to an extent, simply because she was an amazing rider. The show world was crazy in the way that your talent could make you somebody even if you'd come from nothing.

But that was where the similarities in their lives ended. Neither of them would ever have to work a day in their lives if they didn't want to. Julia would earn her Ph.D., go by Dr., and probably only use her degree as a board member of the Museum of Natural History.

She and Bennett would either make horse showing their lives, competing on their family money, or they'd ride for a while and then meet some hedge fund guy, get married, have kids, and become a Real Housewife of New York.

"Zoe, so good to see you." Bennett leaned close and kissed her cheek. Julia followed up with a kiss too.

They made her feel welcome, even if it was all for show.

"Great to see you too," Zoe said.

Bennett and Julia wore classy sundresses with wedge heels. Bennett had pearls on. If they'd gone through the turnstiles like everyone else, they would have looked ridiculous but in the box with the uniformed chefs, they looked appropriate.

Zoe was the one who looked ridiculous. Suddenly she felt young and trashy. She missed the homogenizing outfit of the riding world.

"You're in Bedford now?" Bennett asked.

"Yeah, I'm riding horses for Dakota Pearce and Linda Maro."

"How's Linda doing?" Bennett said. "She worked for Kenny when I was a junior. She was so much fun."

"She's great. She's got a boyfriend now—a nice Irish guy. Eamon—he works for Tiernan Murphy."

"Good for her," Bennett said. "I love Linda. Tell her I say hi. Oh my God, this one time, all of us juniors got so wasted and we were supposed to have a six o'clock lesson and we were like still drunk so we called Linda and she totally covered for us and told Kenny we all had food poisoning. She was so awesome that way."

"Kenny actually believed that?" Nate said. "That's like the horse show equivalent of the dog ate my homework."

Bennett shrugged, jostling her string of pearls. "I guess he did."

"Speaking of being wasted . . . we need drinks," Morgan said.

The bartender poured them cocktails. Zoe asked for extra ice. She would stop at just the one drink but she needed something to take the edge off and she didn't want to stick out.

Zoe actually liked baseball and would have been content to watch the game, but it became clear that while they were *at* the game, they weren't exactly going to be *watching* it.

Zoe typically enjoyed any kind of professional sporting event since she felt she could learn something from the way the athletes approached their sport. She didn't feel that different than a professional baseball player in a way. She even liked the idea of herself as currently in the minor leagues, waiting for her moment to get back to the majors. It made her situation more tolerable.

Nate and Morgan paid attention to an inning here or there, when there was some action, or a big at-bat, but even Morgan didn't seem to care that much. It was true that the Mets' season wasn't off to a great start but Zoe thought it was a little concerning that the heir apparent to the presidency of the club didn't really care about the outcome of the game. Maybe it *was* all about licensing deals.

Every so often Morgan would toss out something about a player that made it clear he was privy to important insider information. "Ramon's contract is up after this season so of course he's hitting the best he's hit in four years," Morgan shared.

"Are you going to pick up his contract?" Nate asked.

Zoe couldn't help but feel a little shiver of excitement at the word 'you.' Morgan got to approve—or would get to approve—multi-million dollar contracts.

"Not sure yet. Need to see if he stays healthy. He's been on the DL thirty games two out of the last three years."

Sometimes Morgan revealed tidbits about the players' personal lives and off-field activities. This always got Bennett and Julia interested.

"What about Matt Hargraves?" Julia asked about the player often photographed out with celebrities.

"He's totally hot," Bennett quickly followed up.

"I know, right?" Julia agreed, but Zoe thought her response seemed forced.

Rumors had swirled for years that Julia was in love with

Morgan. When they were juniors, they'd hooked up once but nothing else had ever happened between them.

"He likes to party," Morgan said. "If you ever see the newspaper say a player has 'flu-like symptoms' that's code word for stayed out too late partying."

"Flu-like symptoms," Julia said. "I love that."

"I wish I had known about that when I was a junior," Bennett added.

Julia laughed. "Yeah, you could have just told Kenny you were having flu-like symptoms."

"I'm still totally going to use that next time I miss the course walk," Bennett said.

"Speaking of course walk, did you see Miranda before the grand prix last week?" Julia's eyes went wide.

"She looked like hell," Bennett added.

"I heard she was partying all night with some guys from the Saudi team," Julia said. "Talk about money. That's a whole different level."

"Yeah, those guys make you look poor," Nate ribbed Morgan.

"Sure," Morgan said, spreading his hands toward the stadium that he owned. "I'm poor."

Zoe felt uncomfortable with both the gossip and the talk of money. They'd probably gossiped about her before, or maybe she wasn't worth gossiping about because she wasn't privileged and wealthy. And they would die if they knew that she only had two-hundred and thirty-three dollars sitting in her bank account right now. That was it. That was all the money she had in the world.

"Tell them about the party at school." Bennett elbowed Julia.

Julia flushed red. "Really?"

"Yeah, come on. You guys have to hear this."

"Well," Julia said, "Have you ever heard of a porn party?"

"I usually watch my porn *alone*," Morgan said.

"Isn't that how everyone watches it?" Nate added.

Julia shook her head. "No, apparently not, because this one guy had this porn party where they show pornos on a giant screen and people sit around and watch them."

"Girls and dudes?" Nate said.

"In the pornos or at the party?" Julia said, her face constantly flushed, either from the topic or the cocktail.

"Both, I guess," Nate replied.

"The movies were regular, like, uh . . ." Flustered, Julia searched for right word.

"Heterosexual?" Morgan supplied.

"Right, heterosexual." Julia giggled.

"I thought you were a smart girl," Morgan said. "But suddenly your vocabulary is down to single syllable words."

"The people at the party were mas-cu-line and fem-in-ine, you mo-ther-fuck-er," Julia said, drawing out the syllables.

Zoe had to give her some credit for the clever comeback.

"I never knew comparative bio programs were that crazy," Morgan said.

"Yeah, seriously," Nate agreed. "I can only imagine what the nuclear physics people are doing."

"Did you go to the porn party, or just hear about it?" Zoe asked.

She hadn't talked that much all night—just a quick comment here or there. She'd been content letting the four of them banter in the way they were clearly used to. Now, though, they were on a topic she felt more comfortable with.

"I just heard about it," Julia admitted.

"Oh no, you're kidding," Morgan said, playfully slapping his thigh with his free hand and nearly spilling the drink he held in his other hand. "I thought you went to it! You just heard about it?"

"Why didn't you go to it?" Nate said.

"Why would I? It sounds . . . I don't know, uncomfortable."

"Have you ever watched porn?" Zoe asked.

"Sure," Julia said quickly.

"Like real porn, not *Showtime* series with lusty sex scenes," Morgan said.

Julia looked rattled. Her face had gone from flushed to bright red. "Well, yes, I mean, like maybe once."

"You've watched porn, right, Zoe?" Nate said.

Nate was looking at her like this whole conversation and thinking of Zoe and porn was giving him a hard-on.

"Of course," she said. Julia and Bennett were probably thinking she was a low class slut but that was because they were jealous that both Nate and Morgan wanted her, not them.

"Next time go to the porn party and report back," Morgan said.

"Or even better, invite us!" Nate said.

Nate and Morgan high-fived. Julia and Bennett rolled

their eyes at them, pretending they were annoyed by their immaturity, but Zoe could tell they really weren't.

At the end of the game, Morgan took them down to the first level of the stadium. Again, security guards greeted Morgan by name. Julia and Bennett exchanged excited glances.

"This never gets old for me," Julia said, seemingly for Zoe's benefit, like it was her way of pointing out she went to games with Morgan all the time.

They wound their way past offices to a large waiting room with more couches and more big screen TVs showing game highlights. Some of the players were already coming out of the locker room with wet, slicked back hair. A reporter with a press pass slung around his neck hurried inside.

"He's usually out about now," Morgan said.

"Who?" Julia said.

But Zoe had a pretty good idea who. Matt Hargraves.

He came out not long after, wearing jeans and a camo T-shirt. He was a big guy up close, with huge forearms full of elaborate tattoos.

Julia and Bennett might have thought he was hot on TV but they were probably scared of him now. Zoe wasn't.

"Morgo!" Matt bellowed when he saw the group.

Zoe wondered what it was like for a player like Matt. He had to know that soon Morgan would be the one running things. Maybe that was why he was so friendly.

"Hargraves, come meet a few of my friends," Morgan said. "They're fans."

Morgan introduced Nate, Julia, and Bennett. Matt offered them smiles but his expression changed when he was introduced to Zoe. He did the quick up-and-down once-over that Zoe was used to. Kind of like a judge does the first time he or she sees a horse come in for a model class.

In a model class you're supposed to stare—not so much in real life, but Matt stared.

Julia and Bennett barely existed—they were the wallpaper now, Zoe could feel it.

"What'cha all doing now?" Matt said.

"We hadn't really made plans yet," Morgan said.

Zoe wondered if there was some rule against hanging out with ownership.

"I'll take this one out for a drink," Matt looked at Zoe a little lecherously. "How 'bout it?"

Julia and Bennett tittered, surprised, maybe slightly offended—definitely relieved.

"You should totally go," Julia said to Zoe. Of course she wanted Zoe to go out with Matt. She wanted her away from Morgan.

"No way, man," Morgan said. "Zoe's with me."

Zoe took that moment to act in a calculated and surreptitious manner. She took a step sideways toward Morgan so he could claim her by putting his arm around her. She leaned into him and said to Matt, "Yeah, sorry, no can-do."

Had she wanted to go out with the baseball player? Not really, actually. Yes, he was hot, but she had her sights set on Morgan.

She had told Linda and Hannah she shouldn't get involved with anyone. But Morgan Cleary wasn't just anyone.

"Sorry, man," Morgan said.

"No worries," Matt said, giving Morgan a sly look. "You two have fun."

"So was that cool to meet him?" Morgan said on the way out of the park.

"He's not as hot in person," Julia said.

"No, not at all," Bennett seconded.

Zoe laughed inside her head. She would have liked to see either Julia or Bennett having sex with Matt Hargraves. They would be so out of their league.

Julia and Bennett called an Uber and Nate said he'd wait with them. They thanked Morgan for the game. He and Zoe headed to the car, Morgan's arm still around Zoe like he'd found her in his CrackerJack box. Zoe knew how proud he felt for beating out Matt for the reward of taking her home tonight.

Let him bask in it, she thought.

She liked feeling desired, feeling wanted.

Sometimes she thought she liked it too much.

Chapter 6

"PREDICTABLE, RIGHT?" Morgan said as he pressed 'P' when they stepped into the elevator.

There was a dim light on in the hall inside the apartment and Morgan didn't bother turning on any other lights. Zoe followed him down a long hallway, past a few doors, to his bedroom. She could only imagine how expensive an apartment like this was. But Morgan's horses cost multiple millions so the fact that he had a place like this wasn't surprising.

"I've been waiting all night for this," he said.

He kissed her forcefully, plunging his tongue into her mouth. Zoe would have preferred a milder approach but she appreciated his desire for her. Sometimes she thought that for her sex was more about feeling desired than desiring someone. He tried to pull her paper-thin shirt over her head and it got stuck.

She reached up to help him maneuver it off but before she could, he decided to pull it in the other direction and tore the neck.

"My shirt," she said.

"It's just a fucking shirt."

"I know but—"

She didn't get to finish her sentence. He turned her so she was facing away from him and pushed her forward a few steps, until she was pressed up against the wall. She took a quick, short breath, feeling a rush of his powerful energy again like she had in the car. She tried to turn around but he held her tight. He pushed harder against her back, grinding up against her with his hips. Her cheek was smooshed up against the fancy wallpaper, which she oddly noted smelled like new money, and her neck kind of hurt from the twisted angle.

Was this sexy, or scary—she wondered? Was this *50 Shades of Grey* and she should be totally turned on, or was this a warning sign that he liked it too rough and was slightly off-kilter mentally?

Finally, he eased off and she was able to turn to face him. He undid his jeans and shrugged out of them. Next her pants came off. He kneeled before her, kissing all over her breasts. She ran her hand through his hair.

The light from the moon slanted through the windows— in the penthouse maybe you didn't have to put your shades down? Or maybe he liked the idea of others watching?

This was more like it—this was sexual territory she'd traversed plenty of times before—and she felt like she was the one in control for a moment since he was on his knees. Although that quickly changed again as he pulled her down to the carpet and pulled off her panties.

"I don't think I saw this before," he said, meaning the tattoo on her hip. It was a constellation of tiny stars. She wished it had more significance than it did. What she had really wanted was the date of her brother's birth, which she had confessed to the guy at the skeazy tattoo place. He had convinced her that stars had more meaning because they symbolized heaven and that it was better than numbers. But Zoe was pretty sure it was just because the stars cost more than numbers. The stars did have one benefit—no one asked what they meant.

And she couldn't have handled telling Morgan about Brayden.

They had already established the first time they'd slept together that she was on birth control. Morgan had been clear to ask. Probably he didn't want any mongrel claims to his wealth. He ditched his boxers and put himself in her. It hurt a little at first and she took another quick breath. That seemed to excite him because he pumped harder and said, "You like it."

It wasn't a question.

He grinded away at her for what seemed like a little too long for her liking. It got boring and while it didn't feel bad, it didn't exactly feel good, either. But a lot of the sex she had had didn't feel good. She hated to admit it but she'd only had a few lovers who really cared about giving her pleasure. She guessed that said a fair amount about her poor taste in men.

She absent-mindedly wondered what sex with Matt Hargraves would have been like. She imagined his tattooed forearms holding himself up over her. Probably he wouldn't have cared about anything but his own dick either.

After a few minutes, maybe sensing that she wasn't enthralled, Morgan grabbed her hair. She looked at him in surprise.

"That kind of hurts."

"I know," he said, pulling harder.

This was where she knew she was supposed to tell him to stop, or even push him away. But she didn't. It didn't seem like the same kind of thing as when Donnie had hit her. That never came during sex. Actually, during sex Donnie was gentle, and he had been one of the few to care about making her climax. It was at the barn that Donnie would put her down and then end up physically hurting her.

This didn't feel like abuse, really.

Yet, it didn't feel quite right either.

But it was Morgan Cleary fucking her and she felt she couldn't forget that. If word got around that they were a thing, wouldn't that prove she was worthy?

So she let him pull her hair. She closed her eyes and tried moaning to get him to come. It seemed to be working. He moved faster and she fake-moaned a few more times, all the while with a clump of her hair in his fist, and finally, he came.

* * *

The next morning Zoe woke before Morgan and walked room to room in the apartment, seeing how the other half lived. It wasn't like it was the first time she'd ever been in an obscenely rich person's house, but the novelty hadn't worn off yet for her.

She quietly admired the floor to ceiling windows in the

living room and the ornate carved pool table in the corner of the room. Crystal bar glasses and bottles of scotch were lined up on the corner bar. She ran her hand over the back of a leather couch and wondered what it would be like to call a place like this home. If she were married to Morgan, she'd hire designers to help her decorate to make it less of a bachelor pad. She let herself indulge in the fantasy for a few minutes. She could have a string of top hunters and her own barn and she could fly to Europe all the time to pick out new prospects. She'd be one of the filthy rich people at the shows who talked about how hard it is to manage their housekeepers, gardeners, and other staff.

She turned when Morgan said, "We better get going." He was showered and dressed, his hair combed back to cover his developing bald spot. "I have a meeting."

"Oh, okay." She took one last look out the windows on the city—it was a view she might not get to see again soon. Now she understood where the phrase, on the top of the world, came from.

She only had the same clothes she had worn the night before including her torn shirt that now instead of resting on the edges of her shoulders, dropped perilously low on one side.

She'd go home, shower and change, then head over to Narrow Lane. If she was a few minutes late, Kirsten would just have to deal.

He didn't offer to make coffee or for them to eat anything before they left. Zoe didn't mind, though. Maybe it was just the horse show life—she was used to getting food on the go, eating most meals with one hand and the other hand on the steering wheel of either a car or a golf cart.

He was wearing a suit without a tie and he looked good in it. The suit was probably custom and cost thousands so it fit well. His loafers were Gucci. Zoe kept herself from asking when she'd see him next. She was determined to play this cool. Too many times she'd tried to badger guys into a relationship. That had never worked. Maybe it was because she always picked the wrong guys, but nevertheless, this time she was going to keep it casual.

She didn't need a relationship now anyway, she reminded herself. She didn't need anyone to distract her from her end goal—landing a job riding good horses. Getting back in the major leagues. If Morgan called her again, cool. If they ended up seeing each other, great. If not, she'd live.

Morgan's meeting was in Bridgeport, where the Mets were considering moving a minor league affiliate, and he'd drop her in Danbury on the way. She thanked him although she had just assumed he would give her a ride back, or order her a car.

A few times in the car ride back to Westchester, she flashed back to the sex they'd had and felt her face heat up. It wasn't burning because it had been hot porno-sex, but because of how rough he'd been with her.

Had he been rough with her the first two times they'd slept together? She didn't think so, but honestly both those times she was bombed out of her mind on booze and drugs. He probably could have tied her up and she wouldn't have remembered.

Morgan kept checking his phone as he drove, often typing

out texts, and Zoe prayed they wouldn't have an accident. She was grateful when traffic slowed them down a few miles from Danbury.

When they came to a standstill Morgan banged the steering wheel. "Fuck!"

"Accident two miles ahead," said his navigation system.

"Shit," he said. "I'm late already. We're meeting with the city to talk about a lease on the park."

Zoe couldn't understand why he hadn't acted more in a rush back at his apartment.

"I can't stop in Danbury now," he said.

"Well, what am I supposed to do? You're just going to drop me on the side of the highway?"

He changed lanes and headed to the next exit.

"No, I'm getting off and I'll drop you somewhere, and then take the back roads around the accident, and get back on the highway north of Danbury."

"There's a deli up the road," she said. "Can you at least drop me there?"

"How far up the road?"

"Not far," she said.

He couldn't even go five more minutes out of his way. He would probably have just left her at the nearest gas station. Zoe closed her eyes briefly. She should have borrowed a shirt from him.

Maybe he sensed her annoyance because he reached out and rubbed behind her neck. "Last night was hot."

"Yeah," she said absentmindedly.

"I'm sorry about your shirt."

But not sorry enough to drive me home, she thought to herself.

The Village Deli always looked closed from the outside, something to do with the darkness of the windows. But people were coming in and out, clutching coffee and the morning paper.

"Bye," Zoe said. She wasn't going to kiss him, which was unlike her. Usually she tried to give a guy a sexy last taste— something to make him want her all over again just as she was leaving. She'd read about doing that a few years ago in some women's magazine and had taken it to heart.

She climbed out of the car. Morgan sped away and Zoe walked into the deli, getting a judgmental look from a mother with a baby and a toddler, probably because her shorts were so short and her T-shirt was torn, and she basically looked kind of like hell.

Zoe didn't shy away from the woman—she stared straight back at her. She wasn't going to shrink away in shame. The fact of the matter was she knew the woman was probably jealous that her days of staying out all night were over. Zoe's torn shirt only proved that she had a crazy night. It didn't look like it was torn on purpose—nope, it was clear it had been a casualty of a long, wild night.

Zoe was feeling better about herself, even if Morgan had just nearly ditched her on the side of the road. Her torn shirt almost felt like some sort of badge of achievement.

That was until she saw John Bradstreet at the counter, getting his coffee.

Then it started to feel like a black mark.

Her first impulse was to run as quickly as possible to the bathroom and not come out until he was gone. But, of course, he had just been handed his coffee and he turned and saw her.

"Whoa, what happened to you?"

"Nothing," she said, trying to adjust her shirt so it didn't slip further.

"Um, your shirt's torn . . ." he pointed to the neck with his coffee.

"I know." She said it ambiguously, leaving room for him to think maybe she'd torn it on purpose—that it was a fashion statement. He was still looking at her with a confused expression.

"I'm, I just . . . I need to go back home and change." She noticed how tall he was—definitely well over six-feet. Too tall for a rider, really.

"You just needed your coffee so bad you had to come out and get it before you put on a not-torn shirt?" he asked.

"Yeah, I know, right?"

Maybe she looked a little unstable, a little close to tears.

"Is everything okay?" John asked carefully.

At least he was being nice to her. Whatever had made him recoil at Narrow Lane seemed to matter less now.

"I actually need a ride back to my apartment. I don't have my car here. Would you have time to drop me?"

"Sure," he said.

"Really? I guess I could call an Uber." She didn't have money for an Uber, though. Or the time to wait for it.

"Of course not. I'll drive you."

In his truck they were officially introduced.

"I'm Zoe Tramell," she said.

"I know who you are," he said as he started the engine. The radio blasted Luke Bryan. Zoe smiled at his choice of music. He reached to turn it down.

"Oh, right, from Kirsten," she said.

"I'll admit, at first I couldn't believe it when she told me you were going to be working at Narrow Lane. She didn't even know who you were."

Which meant he did. Well, of course he did. Everyone knew her—she had been one of the top junior riders. Even if he didn't show at the top shows, he still had read about her or watched her on the live streams.

But did that mean he knew everything else about her too?

He knew the apartment complex where she lived.

"So the ripped shirt—" He took a sip of his coffee and stationed it back in the cup holder. "Dare I ask?"

"You just did ask," Zoe said.

"Okay, true, so do I want to hear the answer?"

"Let's just say I went out last night in the city and things got a little out of hand."

"Okay," he said. "Fair enough. So you're working for Linda and volunteering at Narrow Lane?"

"Yup, that's the state of things."

"Kind of a change for you, right?"

Zoe shrugged. "It's okay," she said, even though it really wasn't. But what was she going to say? She wasn't sure if he knew she was forced to be there doing community service and that no one but Linda would hire her. If he didn't know that, she wasn't going to point it out to him.

She decided to turn the conversation to him. "What about your business . . . Linda said you have a bunch of sales horses?"

"You were asking her about me?" he said, a tiny smile forming on his freckled lips.

"It's pretty boring in this town. I saw a good rider on a cute horse and I wondered what the deal was."

"You just saw me hacking around," he pointed out. "How could you tell I was good?"

"Well, I don't know *how* good you are. But you looked like you could ride a little."

"Not as well as you can."

"I can ride a little," Zoe said, allowing herself a little vanity. "What kind of horses do you have?"

"Some of this, some of that. I've got a pretty nice jumper prospect, a jumper that I think would make a better eq horse. I actually need to show that one to Linda and see what she thinks. I also have a super mare that I think would make a great derby horse."

Zoe straightened in her seat. "Have you shown her much?"

"I did the performance workings on her a few times last summer. She's got an amazing jump."

Zoe's head felt hazy. She needed coffee to think straight but she hadn't gotten any at the deli because she'd been so flustered. She looked longingly at his coffee in the cup holder. "Is there any way I can have a sip?"

"Of my coffee?"

"I'm dying. I need caffeine."

"You were just in a coffee shop."

"I know, just, can I, please?"

"Go ahead. It's black."

"I don't care if it's mud. As long as it's caffeinated mud."
She took the warm cup in her hand. She hadn't even drank
any yet and she already felt better. It was strong. She liked
hers with cream and sugar but it didn't matter. Two sips and
her head was clearer. Back to the derby horse . . .

"So are you going to show that mare in the derbies this
summer?"

"I don't know. I'm not really a hunter rider."

"I am," Zoe said. "I'm a really good hunter rider and I
happen to be right in your backyard."

Zoe saw no reason not to come straight at this. There
wasn't time to waste. She needed horses to show.

"Well, maybe you should come over and sit on her sometime. Tell me what you think."

Zoe took another sip of his coffee. "Great. How about
this afternoon?"

"Wow, that's . . . soon."

"No time like the present," Zoe chirped.

They had pulled up to her apartment complex. The sign
outside read MANOR ESTATES. Why did crappy apartments
always have fancy names? It just made it worse.

"Are you sure you're up for it after your night out?" He
glanced at her torn shirt.

"I'm fine. Believe me, I'm so totally fine."

"Okay, come over after you're done at Linda's. I'll be
around and I won't ride her this morning."

"Great," she said. "I'll see you later."

"Wait," he told her, holding out the coffee. "I think you need this more than me."

Chapter 7

JOHN'S BARN WAS small and sweet. He explained to Zoe when she showed up at three-o'clock that he leased the property from a couple who lived in Manhattan. They had bought the farm for their daughter but her interest in horses had waned and now they only came to the farm infrequently. There was a charming brick house covered in swaths of ivy that sat empty most of the year. He got a break on the lease fee for mowing the lawns and doing general upkeep around the farm and house, essentially acting as the de facto caretaker.

An old dog that looked sort of like a basset hound lay on a dog bed in the aisle.

"That's Harry," John said. "He doesn't move much. You don't have a dog?"

"No," Zoe said as she walked down the aisle.

Sprinklings of shavings and hay dusted the floor. A grooming box cluttered with brushes sat up against the wall. The whole place smelled a little musty and damp but it was kind of a nice smell, like when rain hits asphalt on a hot day.

"I thought all horse people have dogs."

"Most of them do," Zoe said.

"But you don't like dogs?"

"Oh, I love dogs."

It was the one sane choice Zoe had made so far in life—to not get a dog. Not a Jack Russell or a Corgi, or a Danny & Ron's dog. Not even a tiny Chihuahua that could fit in her purse. She knew she wasn't responsible enough to have a dog. Maybe someday she would be able to take care of a dog, but for now she knew she could barely take care of herself.

Zoe walked through the barn, stopping at each horse's stall as John told her about each one, where they had come from, and what he was doing with them. Zoe noticed manure in a few of the stalls. They'd clearly been cleaned—just not continuously picked out.

There was Cruz, the six year-old jumper John thought might end up being an eq horse; Oakley, a five year-old prospect he thought showed the potential to be a high junior/amateur jumper, maybe even a grand prix horse; and Dibs, a five-year-old hunter.

He did most of his business with a dealer in Holland. John didn't go there but instead watched videos and had horses sent over.

The last stall was the mare. A flysheet hung a little lop-sided on her stall door, an errant strap dangling toward the floor. Chunky pink bell boots for turnout (or so Zoe hoped) were velcroed to the blanket hook. The whole barn seemed a little 4-H, but Zoe willed herself not to care.

She went to lean over the stall door, eager to have a look,

nearly giddy with excitement, and John pulled her back. "Careful," he said.

"Does she bite?"

"Yes, sometimes."

"Seriously?" she said.

"No, but she's not exactly America's sweetheart. Mostly she bites other horses if they come too close but so far she hasn't bitten any humans."

"And you bought her why?"

"The price was right and she's fine once you're on her. She's just nasty in the stall. That's partly why I thought she'd make a good derby horse. Some rich owner can watch her win, enjoy her from a distance."

"And never even come to the barn to pat her?"

"You can pat her, she just doesn't really like it. Let me get her out of her stall. She's beautiful to look at."

Zoe looked back at the grooming stall. A broom and shovel leaned against the wall—they didn't hang neatly from wall-mounted hooks like at most of the barns Zoe was used to. "Where are your grooms, or groom anyway?"

"I don't have any."

"What?"

"I have one guy who helps me muck out in the mornings but that's it. I'm a one-man operation."

Zoe blew out a breath. This was getting worse by the minute. A bitch of a mare and a barn with no grooms. She stared straight ahead, unwilling to even look at the mare that John was putting on the cross-ties. Why had she gotten her hopes up?

She heard the snap of the clips on the halter and finally let her gaze fall on the mare.

Okay, she was pretty. She was a beautiful dapple grey. Oh, how gorgeous greys were when they were young! She had a nice slope to her shoulder and a level topline. Her hind end was compact and the angle to her pasterns correct. Her mane and tail were thick and her eye was intelligent.

Her coat gleamed and she was a nice weight. Zoe had to hand it to John—his barn might not be immaculate but his horses looked healthy and fit and that was what counted.

"See," he said.

"Okay, she's well put together." Zoe checked out her legs and hooves, spotting a big splint. "I can see why she's not doing the conformation."

The mare flattened her ears as if she didn't appreciate Zoe criticizing her.

"What's her name?"

"Girl Next Door but we call her Gidget."

"Girl Next Door." Zoe laughed. It was just about the opposite of her. And it was the wrong name for a horse that was barn sour. "Please tell me she doesn't pin her ears when you're on her?"

"Let's get the tack on her and you can see for yourself."

His ring wasn't large and a sprinkler hose was curled up in the corner along with a faded mounting block, a lunge line, a tattered lunge whip, and a few crops.

John got on her first. She wasn't a beautiful mover but Zoe didn't expect her to be. Most derby horses weren't spectacular movers. They were a bit more of a hybrid between a hunter and a jumper. They could jump the moon yet do it in style, they had a huge step, but they didn't typically sweep across the ground pointing their toes.

She did have a really nice canter, which was the gait that counted most in the derbies.

And she did wear her ears nicely. Up and straight ahead like a radar. But none of that mattered if she didn't jump well.

John headed toward a small vertical. She jumped it fine but nothing amazing. Zoe wanted to see amazing. She felt a wave of disappointment—what if John was wrong and his idea of an amazing jump was really just an average jump?

He continued around the simple course that was set up. The jumps were plain, many just standards and rails with the occasional box wall or gate. The highest one was set at maybe three-foot-nine.

John's eye was accurate and his position correct. He was big on the mare but given his height he rode lightly and controlled his upper body—a must for a tall rider. Zoe found herself impressed by his riding. He certainly would fit in on the circuit.

Gidget jumped the highest jump the best of the group, snapping up her knees. John came to a walk and said, "Want to put them up, or you want to get on her now?"

"I'll put a few up," she said. "If you don't mind."

She still hadn't seen anything that took her breath away. Right now the horse was more an average 3'6" horse, and nothing more. With an accurate ride from someone like Zoe she could get ribbons in the derbies but Zoe needed to do more than get ribbons—she needed to win.

"Nope. That's fine."

She raised a vertical-oxer bending line a few holes. "Too high?"

"As high as you want. Just wait."

She returned back to watching from the rail. He picked up a canter and headed to the line. The mare jumped the crap out of both fences this time. Knees snapped up and back rounded. John looked back at Zoe as he turned the corner. "See?"

"Do it one more time the other direction," she said, her heart quickening.

Same thing—form, style, and scope. The mare was six inches over the oxer. Zoe felt goosebumps go up on her forearms. She was itching to ride her and feel her jump herself.

John gave Zoe a leg up, tossing her easily into the saddle. She could have vaulted straight over to the other side. She picked up a trot and soon a canter. She didn't need to waste time. The mare was comfortable to sit on and had a great feel about her. She was naturally balanced, straight, and rhythmic.

Zoe aimed her for one of the smaller jumps. It felt fine—nothing to write home about. Then she turned to the bigger bending line and she felt what she had seen from the ground. The mare had unbelievable power and gave Zoe that ultimate sky bound feeling. John was right after all—she could be a winning derby horse.

"Is she ever spooky?" Zoe said, when she brought her back to a walk. She patted the mare tentatively on the neck.

"No, she's totally brave. She'll jump anything."

"Anything?" Zoe looked around the ring. "Cause these jumps suck."

"I think she'll jump anything. She's never not jumped any-thing."

"We should take her over to Linda's. See what she does over a real course—no offense."

"No offense taken," he said.

"You have a trailer?" she asked.

"Yes, I have a trailer," he said.

Chapter 8

THE NEXT AFTERNOON Zoe told Linda about John's horse.

"Sounds promising."

"Maybe. I just hope he'd let me show her instead of showing her himself. I don't think he knew what he had in the mare and once he realizes how good she is I bet he's going to want to show her."

"I'm not so sure," Linda said.

"Really?"

"I get the feeling he's not really into the showing part."

Zoe couldn't relate. All she ever wanted to do was be in the show ring.

"Can we bring the horse over here and school it? Your jumps are like a world above what he has."

"Of course," Linda said. "Anytime. You don't even have to ask."

"Thanks. Back still killing you?"

"Yeah. My doctor ordered an MRI. I need to go in soon

and get it done." Linda yawned. "I'm sleeping like shit too because I can't get comfortable. And now that I'm not riding, I swear I've like put on ten pounds. Getting old sucks."

"You're not old," Zoe said. "What are you like thirty?"

"Thirty-six."

The bell chimed that signaled a car had driven into the driveway. Soon after, a large SUV pulled up to the barn and Dakota got out. Angelique waved as she drove away.

"Hey there," Zoe called to her. "We were just talking about how Linda's an old fart!"

"You said I wasn't old," Linda said. "I distinctly remember that because for a second I felt better about myself."

"You're not *that* old," Dakota put in. "You're like medium-old."

"Thank you . . . I guess?" Linda said.

Dakota sat down on the tack trunk next to Zoe. She seemed to naturally gravitate toward her, Zoe had noticed. Maybe it was because Zoe was closer to her age or maybe it was because the experience they'd shared in Florida bonded them in a way.

It was only a few hours that they'd spent together when Dakota had been roofied and nearly raped by a polo playing prick but Zoe had been the one who knew all about being roofied since she'd very unfortunately experienced it herself firsthand.

While Hannah was busy warning Dakota to never go out with older men, Zoe was telling her never to drink a cocktail she'd didn't see poured. Zoe didn't expect Dakota to be all innocent and perfect like others did; she was realistic and wanted to save her from making the same mistakes she had at her age.

"Did you see that Chris won the grand prix in La Baule?" Dakota asked.

"Yup, I did. And Mary Beth was fifth."

"Do you think it kills Hannah to see that?"

"Not that Chris won. I know she wants him to do well. But I'm sure it's hard for her to think of him there in Europe with her."

Fernando walked by with Rudi by his side. Today the dog wore a yellow bandana around his neck.

"I feel so badly for her," Dakota said. "I would go crazy with jealousy if my ex-boyfriend I was still in love with was in Europe with his ex-girlfriend who was still in love with him."

"You are so sweet to care about her," Zoe said. "It'll all work out for her. She'll find someone great at school."

"You don't want Chris and her to get back together?"

"I do . . . I mean if it's meant to be. Of course, I do. I'm like a total romantic cheeseball at heart."

"*You're* a romantic cheeseball?" Linda put in.

"Yes," Zoe said. "I love romantic movies. Give me a Nicholas Sparks movie and I'm like all done."

Zoe sat on a box wall in the middle of the ring while Linda taught Dakota on Plato, her up and coming eq horse. Plato was so gorgeous, his stride oiled and smooth. He had a look about him, a presence, that would be a huge asset in the eq ring. It was why Dakota's family had paid so much for him when he hadn't even been to a Final.

Unlike John's unimpressive ring, the ring at Morada Bay

was first class. A four-board fence encircled the ring, which had irrigation and GGT footing.

The jumps were what really made the ring look professional, though. They were bright colors and interesting designs—cut-out walls, geometric designs, and vibrant green roll tops that could have easily been plucked straight from a horse show.

Actually, some of them were. There was a jump with standards in the shape of a butterfly—Plato had taken exception to said standards in a Talent Search class at WEF and so Linda had commissioned an identical jump to practice over at home.

Linda worked Dakota on the flat, asking her to drop her stirrups for much of the flatwork. Zoe liked that Linda didn't go easy on Dakota like some trainers would have. She worked to improve her instead of just telling her all the things she was doing right and stroking her ego.

They warmed up over a few low jumps and then Linda gave Dakota a course. Half-way through the course, Linda said to Zoe, "See how she takes away the distance through the turns? I'm trying to get her to stop doing that."

Zoe nodded—she could see exactly what Linda meant. Dakota would come out of the turn to a jump and sit back in the saddle, taking a hold on the horse, and never letting go. It always resulted in either a deep distance or a weak, long one. When Dakota had finished, Linda called to her to stand in front of them.

"What did you think of that?" Linda asked.

Dakota shrugged. "Kind of okay. I was too deep to the blue oxer and a little long to the red vertical."

"Too deep, too long. Not just to those jumps but to all of the jumps. It's what I've been telling you and I'm going to keep telling you. You need to let go out of the turns. You're coming out of the turn and holding onto his mouth, which takes away his rhythm, and his natural ability to figure out the jumps himself, and it takes away the distance. You're so concerned about finding the right distance that you're actually taking the distance away."

"I know," Dakota said. "I just can't trust it. It's like I come out of the turn and I just grab."

"So don't grab," Linda said. "Do the opposite. Let go. See how it works out. Trust me, it'll be good."

"Try lightening your seat too," Zoe said.

She quickly looked at Linda to make sure she hadn't overstepped her boundaries. Zoe had been hired to ride the horses, not teach lessons. Some trainers were very protective of their title as supreme being and didn't want underlings trying to usurp their power. Usually the less the trainer knew the more protective they were.

Linda was looking at Zoe encouragingly so Zoe continued, "That's what I find works for me. I go through the turn and then lighten my seat a little. Not like a full two-point but just being lighter in your seat bones and then naturally I kind of soften my hands and then just follow the rhythm. The horse gets his eye on the jump and then maybe I sit back down a little bit and ride what's there."

"Good idea," Linda said. "Try it. Go back and do the same course."

Zoe thought about saying, "I hope that was okay," or "I

hope you don't mind that I said that about lightening your seat," but she decided it was clear Linda thought it was fine. Zoe wouldn't suddenly take-over teaching Dakota like she was some kind of co-trainer, but if she saw something every now and then she should feel okay to speak up.

Zoe could see Dakota trying really hard not to pull in the corners of the ring. The first few turns she looked tentative, and the way she got out of the saddle was obvious and mildly overdone. But the girl was doing what she was told. She was listening and trying.

"That's better," Linda said as Dakota came out of the first turn and headed to the in of a line. "Now just ride what you see."

The distance worked out better and Zoe could see Dakota relax just a smidgen. It was working. Each jump was a little smoother and Zoe could tell Dakota was gaining confidence.

"Sometimes you have to just trust something, put your faith in it, and you'll see it'll work out," Linda said when Dakota had jumped the last fence and was circling, waiting to see if she should walk or keep going.

Linda continued, "Keep going and give me the six line the other direction, roll back on the in-and-out, the end-jump and then finish over the broken line. Same thing—out of the turn, lighten your seat, and let your canter take you to the distance. Some horses come out of the turn and they're not straight and you need to correct that but he's straight as an arrow so all you need to do is ride forward and the distance will be there."

Linda nodded along with the jumps. "That's better, huh?" she said to Zoe. "She's getting it. Finally."

"I think she is," Zoe agreed.

"Let him walk, good girl!" Linda called out to Dakota with enthusiasm. "That's good for today. Think about what you just felt. Let that feeling imprint on your brain because that's what I want you to be thinking about every time you're jumping."

Dakota patted Plato. "Thank you," she said to Linda. Then she glanced at Zoe and added, "Thank you, too, that helped about the seat."

"Good, I'm glad," Zoe said.

"Zoe's done a lot of riding and let me tell you, if you didn't already know it yourself, this girl is one hell of a gifted rider," Linda said. "So you're smart to listen when she tells you something."

Zoe felt the warmth of the compliment spreading out through her body. It wasn't that she didn't know she was a good rider. Of course she knew as much. And over her junior career, plenty of people had said it to her and fawned over her. But after a while they'd also become quick to point out any weaknesses, nearly looking to find the chink in her armor. Maybe out of jealousy.

Her life lately hadn't been full of people singing her praises. It felt so good to have Linda recognize out loud that she had knowledge that was worth imparting to others. That she had value to add.

After all the horses were ridden and put away, Zoe found Dakota in Midway's stall, just hanging out with him.

"Besides Logan, this guy was Hannah's fave," Zoe said when she spotted her in there.

"If Midway was human he'd be like the perfect boy-friend," Dakota said. "He'd be loyal. He'd never let you down. He'd never ever cheat on you."

"If he were a guy, would he still be gelded?" Zoe said. "Cause then, yeah, he probably wouldn't cheat on you."

Dakota giggled. "Maybe certain guys should be gelded."

"I'd be in favor of that. I could name a few that could go right to the top of that list."

Dakota snuggled against Midway, rubbing her cheek against his. Zoe was glad to see Dakota had these moments with the horses—that she went in their stalls and cuddled with them. There were plenty of kids on the show circuit who rarely entered a stall. Despite what people might say about her, Zoe wasn't one of them.

She had grown up on her mother's farm riding and taking care of all the ponies and horses. Her mother was most often too harried and too broke (not to mention too drunk) to give Zoe much attention. Zoe started going into the barn at night at an early age, when her mother had passed out on the couch. She would visit her favorite horses, pressing her face against their soft coats.

If some kids were raised by wolves, she had been raised by horses. It was in their stalls late at night when the barn was quiet that she felt loved. Sure, as she'd grown up and gotten to be the kind of rider who was asked to show multiple horses a day, she didn't have as much time for tacking them up or going into their stalls.

But she loved them because they had loved her. They had given her a safe place when she hadn't had one.

She was pretty sure Dakota was in Midway's stall for the very same reason. In a way, she was being raised by horses too.

"Is there a particular boy we should be gelding?" Zoe said now. "Or is it just boys in general?"

"A particular boy."

Zoe went into the stall. "Go ahead, lay it on me."

"You don't want to hear about my crap," Dakota demurred.

"Why wouldn't I? Come on, spill."

"I got together with this guy. But then I get a text from a friend that at Camden he was with another girl."

"He's a horse guy?"

"Yes."

"Do I know him?"

"Parker Zalme."

"Parker? He's cute."

"Yeah, I know." Dakota held out her palm and Midway licked it like he was a dog.

"He's also quite a few years older than you."

"I know that too."

"And he's a *total dick*!" Zoe widened her eyes for emphasis. "You knew that too, right?"

Dakota shrugged. "I guess, maybe, I don't know."

"Come on," Zoe said. "Parker Zalme? There are good guys and there are bad guys. If you go after the bad guys you have to expect them to be bad. Not to change for you because they've finally seen the light and fallen in love. Leave that to the Nicholas Sparks movies."

Dakota looked down at the shavings and Zoe worried

she'd been too harsh with the girl. But Dakota picked her eyes up and challenged Zoe with her stare, "Look who's talking. Aren't you the queen of the bad boys? I mean, Donnie?" Dakota made a show of cringing.

"Yeah, that was a big mistake but things get more complicated as you get older."

"So when you were my age you only hung out with good guys?"

"No, not exactly," Zoe admitted. "I have been known throughout my life to have pretty horrible taste in the opposite sex. But here's the thing—maybe I can save you from making the same mistakes I made."

"And how are you going to do that?"

"Won't just warning you and telling you to learn from my life work?"

"Somehow I doubt it."

Both were silent and contemplative for a few moments. Midway lowered his head and searched the shavings for any overlooked pieces of hay.

"What if we make a pact?" Dakota offered.

"What kind of pact?"

"Like neither of us can go after, or hook up with, any assholes."

"Define asshole?" Zoe said.

"Do I really have to?" Dakota said. "Basically we can't go after any of the guys we usually go after. If we're into a guy he has to be a nice, loyal, kind, sweet guy."

"To put it in horse terms we can only go after Midways," Zoe said. "No Platos."

Plato was gorgeous and talented and cocky. He was also

unpredictable at times, which was why Dakota hadn't shown him yet. Linda planned for her to start using him this summer and save Dudley for important classes and the finals. The thing about horses, though, was that over time some of them could learn to be dependable. Unlike men.

"How will we keep tabs on each other?" Zoe asked.

"Well, it's more like an honor system but I guess there's always HorseShowDrama."

"Okay. You're on." Zoe reached out and shook Dakota's hand. It felt oddly formal. She wasn't even sure why she was agreeing to all this. Could a pact with a fourteen year-old seriously make her stay away from jerks?

"The only problem is that most of the horse show world seems to be filled with dicks," Dakota said.

"There is that," Zoe agreed.

Dakota shrugged. "At least I've got my boyfriend, Middie."

"I'm sorry, he's my boyfriend." Zoe reached for Midway possessively.

"Haha," Dakota said, encircling Midway's nose with her arm and kissing him. "This one is all mine.

Chapter 9

ON FRIDAY, John brought Gidget over to Morada Bay. Zoe was impressed that John's trailer wasn't a two-horse; it was a four-horse gooseneck. It was by no means new but it did actually match his black truck. Zoe helped him unload the mare. She came off the ramp looking bored, which Zoe noted was a good sign. To really be a derby horse, she had to be brave as the day was long and not care about anything, especially new settings or spooky jumps.

Her first real test was the flock of guinea hens, which were pecking the grass near the barn. Gidget took one look at them and sighed.

They brought Gidget into the barn and Zoe helped John tack her up.

"I didn't know you do things like tack up a horse," he said. "I guess I thought riders like you just hop on at the ring."

"Riders like me? What does that mean?"

John backtracked. "Like top riders. Riders that win at the biggest shows. That's all I meant."

"Maybe not all of us know how to tack up but some of us do," Zoe said. "I don't exactly come from royalty in case you haven't guessed."

Zoe put the baby pad on Gidget's back. Then she positioned the half-pad.

If she came from royalty, she sure as hell wouldn't be in the situation she was right now, trying desperately to get back on her feet and get back in the show ring.

"I'm sorry. I'm being kind of a dick." John slid the saddle onto Gidget's back. "I guess I just feel kind of inferior to you."

Zoe buckled the girth on the side opposite John and then came around to the other side where he was standing. "Inferior to me? Why?"

"Cause you've been there, done that. Champion at all the best and biggest shows. WEF, Indoors."

"You ride really well too," Zoe said, pulling the girth up a few holes.

John unhooked the mare from the cross-ties. "But I haven't done everything you have and I'm self-conscious about that."

Zoe handed him the bridle. "Did you want to do all that, or do you? I guess I assumed you liked the sales side of things."

"There was a time when I would have killed to show at all the big shows. I'm not really sure anymore. I do like the sales aspect. Seeing something in a horse and bringing it along . . . ."

Linda limped out of the office toward them with her little dog, Taffy, toddling behind her. "I'm ready to see this horse go," she said, stifling a yawn.

"I asked Linda to watch her too," Zoe said, by way of explanation.

She hoped John wasn't offended but she wanted an extra set of eyes on the mare. Linda could be a reality check and could tell Zoe if she was insane for thinking this mare might have what it took to be a winning derby horse.

Taffy yipped, looking up beseechingly at Linda.

"I'm sorry, I can't pick you up, sweetie," she said.

"Back still hurting?" John said.

"Killing," she said.

John did up the noseband and offered the reins to Zoe.

Zoe took the reins. "You don't want to ride her first?"

He shook his head. "You rode her great. I don't see the point in me hopping on her."

Zoe shrugged. "Okay."

Out in the ring, Linda and John stood together in the middle while Zoe warmed up Gidget. She couldn't hear what Linda and John were saying and it drove her a bit crazy. They were probably just chit-chatting but Zoe wondered if they were talking about her.

She cut across the ring a few times to try to catch what they were saying but didn't want to be too obvious. The only thing she heard was Linda saying it hurt her back less to stand than to sit.

When the mare was loosened up, John lowered an oxer so Zoe could start over it. After a few times, he raised it back up.

Zoe said, "I guess I'll just jump around at this height first?"

"Sounds good," Linda said. "Let's see her do her thing."

Zoe kicked the mare into a canter and jumped around the

course. The jumps were only three-foot-six and Gidget was good over them, but not spectacular. That wasn't necessarily a bad thing. Horses that had a lot of scope often didn't try much over the smaller jumps.

Not once did Gidget spook—not even at the weird butterfly jump. A lot of the jumps were more equitation or jumper style and sometimes horses would actually spook at a big natural log jump more often than they would at colorful rails since they'd seen more of those in their life. But it was a start anyway. So far Gidget was proving to be as brave as John had promised.

Linda and John put the jumps up a few holes and lengthened the lines a few inches so they wouldn't be tight for the mare given the height of the jumps. They were solid four-foot now. But some of the derby jumps even went up to four-foot-six.

Zoe circled Gidget at the canter. She breezed around the course, carrying a little more pace this time. Over the first jump she felt it. That amazing power off the ground. It only got better as she continued.

When she finished, Linda wolf-whistled.

"Right?" Zoe said. "She jumps the shit out of them, doesn't she?"

Linda turned to John. "Where the hell have you been hiding this horse?"

"I haven't been hiding her. I showed her a few times. But I guess if you're not a rider like Zoe no one notices."

"Well, now you've got a rider like Zoe."

"Do I?" John said, looking at Zoe.

Zoe grinned. "If you want me, you've totally got me."

"I do," he said.

* * *

"I need you to lead today," Kirsten said to Zoe.

"Lead?"

"Lead. One of our walkers is sick. I need you to fill in."

"Oh," Zoe said ambivalently as she finally understood what Kirsten meant. She meant Zoe couldn't whip out of the barn before that first mini-van pulled in. She meant Zoe was going to have to be actually involved in a lesson.

"Tack up Daisy and bring her into the ring," Kirsten told her.

"Wait, what kinds of things do I need to know?" Zoe felt completely unprepared for this, which since it had to do with horses was a totally new feeling for her.

"I'll give you the quick rundown when you get her into the ring."

Zoe felt more nervous as she tacked up Daisy than she had before going into the Medal Finals. What if the girl or boy had spasms or drooled? What if he or she looked contorted? Zoe didn't know how she would be able to handle it.

She was squeamish when she passed someone on the street in a wheelchair or with some other disability. She didn't even particularly like old people. They kind of freaked her out. That was partly why she liked the horse show world. It was so insular and full of beautiful, healthy people.

A well-known trainer had suffered a stroke during Florida and was now recovering and photos and videos of her circu-

lated all over social media asking for donations. Like too
many trainers she had no health insurance or savings. Every
time one of the images came up on Zoe's news feed, she
quickly swiped past.

She felt shaky as she led Daisy into the ring and she wondered if she should tell Kirsten that she was feeling sick, or
that she just couldn't do this part. She was about to say something when John walked into the ring with Kirsten. It caught
her so off guard to see him there and she forgot about her
nerves for a moment.

"Zoe, this is John Bradstreet. He'll be the other walker.
John, this is Zoe Tramell."

Zoe said, "We know each other already."

"Okay," Kirsten said. "John will walk next to Molly.
Zoe, your job will be to lead Daisy. Keep her walking
straight."

"That's it?"

"Basically, yes," Kirsten said.

Zoe had more questions flying through her head. What if
Molly fell off? What would Molly look like? What would be
wrong with her?

Her nerves had returned.

She heard car tires crunching on the gravel driveway.
Soon Molly, whoever she was, would be here. Daisy blew out
a huge breath onto Zoe's arm. Zoe was grateful for the distraction. She fidgeted with Daisy's bridle, making sure the
keepers were all tidy.

Molly and a woman who was either her mother or her
caregiver appeared in the doorway. Kirsten greeted them
warmly.

Molly wasn't in a wheelchair. She was walking, albeit with a lot of help from the woman. She walked behind Molly, her chest pressed against Molly's back, her arms hooked under Molly's, basically holding her upright. Molly took jerky steps, her muscles clearly not doing what they were supposed to. Zoe noticed how skinny and atrophied her legs were.

Zoe thought she would feel a bolt of disgust but instead she felt nothing but awe. Awe for Molly and how hard it must be for her not to be able to walk on her own.

With the woman's help, Molly made it up to the mounting block. John signaled to Zoe to lead Daisy over.

"Hi, Molls," he said and Molly replied, "You again?"

Kirsten said, "Molly, we have a new helper today, Zoe. Zoe, this is Molly and her mother, Joanne."

"Hi," Zoe said. So it *was* her mother. Zoe felt tears nearly pressing at her eyes. Here was a mother so dedicated that she held her daughter while she walked. There were certainly dedicated mothers she saw at the horse shows—not her own, of course. But the horse show mothers sometimes seemed more devoted to winning than to their children.

Would those horse-show moms be like Joanne if they had a daughter like Molly?

"Hi," Molly said and smiled a little crookedly at Zoe, some of the muscles in her face frozen. Still, her smile was bright and infectious. Zoe felt instantly at ease. This was going to be all right after all.

John and Kirsten helped Molly mount Daisy. Molly looked more relaxed the moment she was in the saddle, like she was a creature that needed to be on horseback.

Joanne stepped away as Kirsten talked to Molly.

"How's your day going?"

"Okay."

"Ready to work hard today? Work on your core? And have some fun?"

Molly nodded.

"Okay, let's go out to the rail."

Molly and Kirsten talked much of the time that Molly rode. Zoe had assumed therapeutic riding was basically like a pony ride—a few times around in each direction and then get off. But she soon learned it was not that different than a typical riding lesson.

Kirsten was as or more skilled than a typical instructor and worked on Molly's position and body control. She had her put her arms out to the sides and lean forward to touch different parts of the saddle. Then she had Molly steer Daisy in and out of cones and play a game of red-light-green-light. John walked next to her the whole time, sometimes touching her leg or hands to help demonstrate what Kirsten was explaining.

Zoe was surprised at how quickly the lesson went by. She'd figured every minute would feel like forever but a quick glance at the clock in the ring showed it was already half over.

Kirsten had Molly wait in the middle of the ring while she attached what looked like laminated photographs onto different spots on the walls of the arena with velcro.

"Who's your favorite singer or band?" Molly asked Zoe.

"Me?" Zoe was taken aback that Molly was talking to her. "Um, maybe Blake Shelton or Luke Bryan."

"Luke Bryan?" Molly said. "My brother likes Luke Bryan."

"Who's your favorite?" Zoe asked.

"I like Carrie Underwood and Beyoncé. But my favorite favorite favorite is Taylor Swift. You're really pretty."

Zoe's face flushed red. Not at being called pretty necessarily but at being told she was pretty in front of John. How was she supposed to respond? Was she supposed to deny it? She decided to say, "Thank you. That's so sweet."

Zoe had thought the talk about music was pretty random but it turned out the photographs Kirsten was pinning up on the walls were of singers. Kirsten came back into the middle of the ring and then instructed Molly to go find Christina Aguilera.

Molly jostled Daisy with her lower leg and tried to direct her with an outstretched hand but Zoe had to help her maneuver Daisy toward her destination. The first photo wasn't Christina, but Beyoncé. It took two more stops to find Christina. Then she had to find Gwen Stefani and back to Beyoncé before Kirsten announced she needed to find Taylor Swift.

Molly's face lit up. She had pretty blue eyes, freckles, and dark hair that was pulled back in a ponytail under her helmet. "Taylor!"

"I like her music too," Zoe said. Mostly Zoe liked the songs about Taylor's troubled relationships. She could identify with the girl on that level.

When they found Taylor's photo, Molly leaned forward in the saddle. John moved with her, just in case, shadowing her.

"You kind of look like her," Molly said. "You're both super super pretty!"

"You are really making my day," Zoe said. "You're making me feel so good about myself!"

It was kind of sad but honestly Zoe hadn't had so much praise or attention in a long while. It *was* making her feel good.

"Don't you think she's super pretty?" Molly said to John.

"Taylor Swift?" John said.

"No, Zoe."

Now, Zoe's face was bright red. She looked at Daisy's hooves, hoping John might not notice her blushing. The moment until he spoke felt long, as she wondered how the hell he was going to respond.

"Both are super pretty," John said. "But not as pretty as you, Molls."

Molly cocked her head to the side and smiled broadly at John.

Now, look who's sweet, Zoe thought to herself.

At the end of the lesson, Joanne appeared back in the ring. John and Kirsten helped Molly dismount. Joanne immediately took her position behind Molly again.

"Mom," John said. "Do you want me to help her out?"

Mom. Zoe's head spun. *Mom.* Joanne was John's mom?

Zoe registered Joanne's black hair and fair complexion. The fact that she was tall, probably around five-foot-ten.

If Joanne was his mom, Molly was his sister.

My brother likes Luke Bryan.

Zoe remembered the Luke Bryan playing in John's car.

Shit. No wonder John had been so upset when Zoe had insulted Pepper for being an Appy and generally acted like Narrow Lane was beneath her.

"I'm fine, sweetie," Joanne said. "See you later."

"Bye John, bye Zoe," Molly called.

Zoe waved and smiled but she felt like she might throw up. She was such an ass.

In the barn, she untacked Daisy, glad to have something to do.

When John came in, she said, "I had no idea you—" She didn't even know how to finish her sentence, which made her feel like even more of an ass.

"That my sister has cerebral palsy? Yup, she does."

"I was such a jerk that day I said that stuff about Pepper. Now I'm starting to see how important these horses are."

"They're important all right," John said.

"I'm really, really sorry," she said again.

"It's okay," John replied. "It's certainly not the first time anyone's been insensitive."

Zoe cringed at the word insensitive, even though that's exactly what she had been.

Chapter 10

ZOE MUST HAVE DONE a decent job leading because Kirsten asked her to lead more often. Zoe was nervous again the next few times but soon she became completely comfortable with the different kids and their different disabilities. She got used to seeing their parents help them out of the car and to the ring. She even learned how to work a motorized minivan ramp.

The kids all had their different personalities. Zoe felt really stupid for having somehow assumed they'd be anything other than regular kids. Sure, it was painful sometimes to see a kid who had so many challenges in life. But it made her realize how lucky she was and how she couldn't afford to mess up her own life.

The horses allowed the kids to do things they usually weren't capable of. Some of the kids could do more than others. Some could trot and one could canter. Others could only walk, but still Zoe could see how relaxed they were once they were in the saddle.

One of the kids she led often was mostly non-verbal. On the day he clearly said Daisy's name out loud, Zoe teared up.

After that lesson, she'd gone into Daisy's stall, pressed her face against her coat, and full-on cried.

Kirsten had found her there.

"I'm not even sure why I'm crying exactly," Zoe said. "It was just so amazing. You heard him, right? He clearly said Daisy."

"I go home and cry like three days a week."

Zoe wiped away her tears and a little of Daisy's hair that was now plastered to her face. When Kirsten left her alone again, Zoe whispered to Daisy, "He said your name. Did you hear it? You are amazing. You are the best."

The next time Zoe spoke to her counselor she told her how grateful she was to be working at Narrow Lane—how she felt it was making her a better person.

Zoe learned that just like with regular kids, she had her favorites. Of course Molly topped the list. John helped out plenty of days, not just with Molly. He seemed to have fully gotten over how she'd acted that first day they'd met at Narrow Lane.

"Why the hell didn't you tell me John's sister rides at Narrow Lane?" she'd asked Linda the day after finding out.

"I didn't tell you that?" Linda said.

"No, you didn't, and I totally put my foot in my mouth in front of him."

Linda shook her head. "I'm telling you, I can't sleep so it's like I'm not even thinking straight most of the time. I'm sorry."

It wasn't as if Zoe and John could hold amazing conversations as they worked together during a lesson at Narrow Lane, but just being in close proximity to him was something Zoe came to look forward to.

One time after a lesson finished up, Zoe got up the courage to ask him more about Molly. "I don't know much about muscular dystrophy," Zoe said. "Is it something you're born with?"

"You mean cerebral palsy?" John said.

"Oh God, yeah. I just got the two confused. I should have known the difference."

Here she was trying to be sensitive in how she asked and instead she had solidly inserted her foot in her mouth. Again.

"Don't worry about it," John said. "It's not like I would have known much about it either if I hadn't had Molly for my sister and then started helping at Narrow Lane."

Zoe wanted to ask him if he would have volunteered at Narrow Lane if Molly wasn't his sister. Basically she wanted to figure out how saintly he was.

"So cerebral palsy is usually something you're born with although sometimes you can't see it right away," John said. "I think with Molly they started to know pretty early because she had problems swallowing. She still does. But mostly the muscle problems affect the way she moves. Some kids with CP have seizures but we're lucky because Molly doesn't. We're also lucky that she doesn't have neurological symptoms."

"That's good," Zoe said, but then felt stupid again. Could there be anything good about having CP?

"How do you get it?" she asked.

"You don't always know. It could be from premature birth or an infection during pregnancy. My mom didn't have any of those so we don't really know what happened or why she has it. I know my mom feels like somehow she did something wrong."

"That's awful." Zoe thought of her own mother. Surely she had blamed herself for Brayden's death and it had eaten away at her, making her basically unable to care for Zoe. After all, her mother should have kept a better eye on him. You don't let a five year-old wander all around a farm unsupervised, especially a farm with large animals and a pond. Sometimes Zoe couldn't decide what made her more angry—that her mother had let Brayden drown, or that after his death she wasn't much of a mother to her.

"I know." John looked contemplative, like it was something he thought about often.

But what could he possibly do about it? What could anyone do about it? When she'd first met John she'd assumed his life was near perfect with a perfect little happy family. She tended to assume that about most people. But the truth seemed to be that every family had its own pain. There was John's family with Molly's CP. And there was Dakota with her absentee parents. Also Hannah with her anxiety-plagued mother.

"I wish my mom didn't blame herself in any way but I'm sure she does," John said.

"She's so good with Molly. She's amazing."

"She is," John said. "And my dad too. They've never

stopped trying to give Molly the best possible life and they never will."

Zoe felt her throat getting thick. How would her life have been different if she'd had parents that cared about her as much as John's and Molly's parents clearly cared about them? But could she fully blame her mother after losing her son?

John's experience with Molly made him good with the kids at Narrow Lane, or maybe he was just a natural at it. Either way, he was always ready with a steadying hand when they needed it. Somehow he seemed to anticipate what they'd need long before it was visible but he also didn't overdo it; he didn't come to their aid unnecessarily, which would make them feel weak.

One day, Zoe was leading a girl she'd never led before, Sara, when Sara reached out and grabbed Zoe's hair. Completely surprised, Zoe yelped. John helped gently pry Sara's fingers from Zoe's hair.

"Oh yeah," he said casually. "Sara does that sometimes."

He took off the ball cap he was wearing and handed it to her. "You might want to put this on."

Zoe looked at Sara's face—old Zoe would have been furious at the teenager. But she strangely couldn't find any anger inside of herself. She knew it wasn't Sara's fault.

"I'm putting on the hat," she said to Sara as she accepted it from John and tugged it over her head. "My hair is one of my prize possessions and I can't afford to lose it, or I'll never get a date!"

Sara stared straight ahead. She didn't seem connected to the world around her. When she was on the ground she made all sorts of noises and grunts and sometimes flapped her arms—in the saddle she was controlled and peaceful.

"Let's get back to work," Kirsten said to them all, and Zoe could see Kirsten was trying to contain her smile.

Had she known that Sara would pull Zoe's hair and she hadn't said anything? Had both Kirsten and John known? He did seem quick to offer his hat, like he knew the drill.

After the lesson was over and Zoe was untacking Daisy, John and Kirsten came into the barn.

"Sorry about the hair pulling," Kirsten said. Now she was full-out smiling.

"You knew that was going to happen, didn't you?" Zoe said.

John chuckled, which was her confirmation.

"Thanks a lot, guys. I guess I better be on my guard from now on."

"No, definitely not," Kirsten said. "We'll tell you if you need to know anything about anyone else, I promise. Right, John?"

"Definitely," he said. "We just couldn't resist. Do you hate us now?"

"No, I just might never trust you again."

Zoe wasn't actually mad at them. It felt kind of like the pranking that members of a sports team might do. The harmless kind that built rapport. If anything, Zoe felt like maybe they were coming to accept her, to see her as one of the team. Maybe this had been her initiation and now she was one of them.

"We owe you a drink," John said.

"Definitely," Kirsten said. "At least one drink, maybe two. How hard did she get you?"

Zoe touched her hair. "She took out a decent clump."

"Two drinks, it is," John pronounced.

Chapter 11

WHAT HAD ONCE BEEN a sleepy Westchester town with a quaint center consisting of only a handful of stores was now a bustling New York city suburb with an elongated main street and chain stores grouped on intersecting streets. The Episcopal church with its pretty front yard, the old playhouse, and a few other original buildings still lent the town a sense of its place in history.

At one point, there had been a thriving group of fox hunters in the town but the hunt club had disbanded a few years ago, sending its remaining hounds to adoptive homes. The rustic tavern that the members of the hunt frequented was now refurbished into a toney pub with exposed brick walls and framed photos of prominent sports figures, including a few race horses.

"Show jumping just never gets its due," Zoe said as she walked in with John and Kirsten and glanced over the shots of baseball players, basketball players, football players, soccer players, and even a few boxers. "I mean when you think about it, there are actual Olympic riders who live around here and are their pictures up on the wall? No."

"It's a good point," John said. "I guess I'd never really thought about it before."

It felt a little strange being somewhere other than the barn with them, but it wasn't an altogether unfamiliar feeling for Zoe. It was the way it went with horse people. You formed your friendships in the barn aisles or at the in-gate and then over time that led to dinners at restaurants or outings to the mall or spa on off days.

Those first times out together in real clothes always were slightly uneasy, as if you needed to figure out who a person was out of the show world. A girl who felt confident in the show ring could be shy and reserved outside of it, and vice-versa.

Kirsten looked a little smaller, a little softer outside of Narrow Lane. They ordered a round of drinks and sat together at a table constructed from an old keg barrel.

Zoe had gone over how to deal with social drinking with her counselor.

"I'm not an alcoholic," she had told her counselor over the phone.

"True, but you have a history of substance abuse and alcohol abuse. And you take medication for bipolar disorder."

"Wow, you make my life sound so rosy."

"I'm just trying to mirror the facts for you."

"Mirror, mirror on the wall . . ." Zoe trailed off. "So I can have one drink? Just so I don't stick out?"

"There's no exact rulebook. You have to learn to know

yourself and what you can handle. You might very well find you can't drink at all."

John raised his glass. "To surviving a hair-pulling!"

They clinked glasses.

"You know, I really thought I was going to hate working at Narrow Lane." Zoe gave a quick sidelong glance at Kirsten, to make sure she wasn't offended. She'd already tempered what she really had felt, which was that at first she *had* hated working at Narrow Lane. "I mean, I just didn't understand how important therapeutic riding is. I guess I was just scared and worried about what I was going to see and that was really stupid."

"A lot of people feel that way," Kirsten kindly offered. "It's a pretty normal feeling."

"But the work you do is amazing." Zoe looked at Kirsten meaningfully. "Really, it's amazing."

"Thank you." Kirsten straightened in her seat like she was really pleased. "That means a lot coming from you. John told me all about how accomplished a rider you are. I don't really follow horse showing at all."

Horse showing—the way she referred to it drove home just how much Kirsten didn't know about Zoe's world. It was funny how two people could work with horses but have completely different experiences.

"It's great that you're branching out and seeing these kids with the horses," Kirsten added. "I'm sure it's off-base but show people kind of have a reputation for being elitist assholes."

"Some are elitist assholes," Zoe said, laughing. She was

glad to deflect the conversation away from her 'branching out' because of course she hadn't exactly branched out voluntarily. Something Kirsten knew since every week she had to sign her timesheet. But something John might not yet know. "But some people are really great and do a lot of charity work."

"I guess it's just like any world—all kinds of people," John put in.

Zoe asked Kirsten how she got into riding. She told her how she'd started at a local lesson barn and then had gotten involved with Pony Club, working up to earning her C-2 rating.

"I'm sure all the things I've done would sound crazy to you," Kirsten said. "You've probably never been out of a ring."

"Hey now," Zoe said, trying to make light of the obvious chip on Kirsten's shoulder. "Actually I grew up on a farm with acres to ride over and a pond where we'd take the ponies swimming."

Zoe caught herself, feeling the familiar closing of her throat. She was almost transplanted back to that awful day that changed her life forever. The feel of her pony underneath her as she rode bareback around the pond shouting Brayden's name till her voice hurt. Then, later, the emergency responders searching the water. Eventually the ambulance pulling out silently.

She never took her ponies swimming again.

"Well, I'm glad to hear you're different than a lot of the horse show people," Kirsten said.

So many people that rode in other disciplines or showed

only locally thought all show circuit riders could do was ride perfectly prepared horses around eight jumps set in straight lines. Yes, it was true of some percentage of the circuit but not all. Yet, Zoe didn't have the energy to try to explain more of that to Kirsten. Not now.

More people entered the pub, stopping in for a drink or bite to eat after work. Soon it had that nice amount of noise, enough to make a place feel popular but not so loud you couldn't talk without screaming.

After she finished her drink, Kirsten said she really had to get home. Her kids would be waiting for help with homework and her husband had probably burned dinner.

Zoe could tell this was a stretch for Kirsten—that she didn't usually stray from her routine of Narrow Lane and her home life. She felt oddly touched that she'd even come out for a drink at all.

Zoe wasn't sure whether this meant she and John should leave too. She moved to get up when Kirsten did and Kirsten said, "We said two drinks. Don't leave because of me."

John made no movement toward leaving so Zoe sat back down. She'd only drank a quarter of her drink, pacing herself. Kirsten left a twenty-dollar bill on the table and said good-bye, and that she'd see them the next day.

"She's nicer than I thought when I first met her," Zoe said, after she'd gone. "I guess a lot of my first assumptions were wrong."

"Kirsten's really great. She doesn't exactly rake it in doing what she does but she loves it and she's so good with the kids."

"She really is," Zoe agreed.

"You're pretty good with them too," John said. "Molly really likes you."

"I like them a lot. I never thought I would. I mean I like helping kids in the show world and so I guess it's not that different. I used to love helping Jamie with the pony kids and I really like helping Linda with Dakota."

"Maybe you should be a trainer. Have a barn full of pony kids."

"I don't know. I also love to show. I don't think I could give that up and to be a really great trainer you kind of need to do just that. What about you? Do you ever want to have customers?"

"I'm not sure. Maybe someday."

"You'd have to go to more shows. Why don't you go to more now?"

John fiddled with his glass. "I haven't really had the right horses."

"That doesn't stop most people."

John laughed. "That's true but I only want to be in the ring if I have a chance. I don't want to make a fool out of myself."

"Young horses guarantee you'll make a fool out of yourself. Plus, even the best riders totally mess up sometimes."

"You can say that because you're *one* of the best riders . . . it's easy for you to say it's not a big deal to mess up . . ."

"I don't think anyone would say I'm one of the best riders right now. I haven't been in a show ring for weeks."

John didn't ask if she wanted another drink. Maybe he

knew about her history. Or maybe the two drinks thing had just been metaphorical.

Either way, Zoe was grateful because thinking back about the pond and Brayden was making her really want to have another. And then another. And another. She really wanted to get wasted. To make the thoughts in her head go away.

"I feel like we didn't really show at the same shows as juniors . . . who did you ride with again?" Zoe said. Maybe if she kept talking to him, the suffocating feeling she had would go away.

"We showed at the same shows sometimes. You just don't remember me," John said.

"Really? I think I'd remember you if we had."

"I wasn't very good."

"First of all, I find that hard to believe. And second of all, girls at the shows—we notice guys. Every single one of them. They kind of stick out."

"I rode with Kelly Saver. Do you know her?"

Zoe shook her head.

"She's more of a local trainer. We did some of the same shows you did, like Vermont, but we were basically nobodies."

"That's not a very nice way to talk about yourself," Zoe pointed out.

"It is what it is. Kelly was a good trainer but it was more of a local program and my family didn't have any money."

"Did you do the eq or what?"

"I did a little bit of everything. I rode whatever she had for me. I never owned my own horse. My parents couldn't afford it. I qualified for all the eq finals my last year but the horse I rode was really green. My biggest claim to fame was winning the Connecticut Junior Medal Finals."

"Well, that's something."

"Not compared to everything you've won."

"You know I like pretty much choked my last year at all the eq finals, right?"

"You were fifth in the Medal. That's pretty good to me."

Zoe couldn't help but be surprised that he knew exactly what ribbon she'd gotten. "I was the kid who was supposed to *win* one of the finals. I'm sorry if it sounds like bad sportsmanship but fifth was nothing. Everyone knew I choked."

"I get it," he said. "But fifth still doesn't sound bad to me. I was on the stand-by for a while for the Medal Finals my last year and that was like amazing to me. Kelly didn't have kids go to the Medal Finals to begin with. Usually when someone got good enough they'd leave her."

Zoe thought about it. It was true that she ran in such circles of the horse show world that she got spoiled. That it was win or nothing. That fifth in the Medal Finals felt like an epic fail.

It was healthy for her to be around someone like John and gain some valuable perspective. But at the same time if she wanted to be the best she couldn't be happy with low ribbons or just making the stand-by for a while.

"Why didn't you leave Kelly? I'm sure some other trainer would have taken you on as a working student. Especially since you're a guy. I actually can think of a few trainers who would have *loved* to get their hands on you." She widened her eyes, intimating nefarious behavior.

John shuddered. "You're skeeving me out."

"But seriously, you never got any trainers coming up to you at shows?"

"Maybe once or twice. But it wasn't really in the cards for my family." John took a sip of his beer. "This one time in Vermont, Kelly actually had a nice sales horse. I showed it in the junior hunters and she had me do the derby and I laid down this crazy good first round. I got a better score than you and I came back on top for the handy round, against all the professionals and you, and you were basically like a professional, even back then."

"What year was this?" Zoe tried to think back but a class that stuck out to John was just one of a million classes she'd ridden in as a junior.

"It was my last junior year, so three years ago."

She shook her head. "I'm not remembering. Anyway, what happened? Did you win?"

"No. I didn't do the hand gallop. I'm bad at hand gallops. I don't go forward enough. You nailed the hand gallop and the rest of the course and you won."

"What'd you finish up?"

"Sixth. It was great ribbon for me."

"But you could have won!"

"I know."

Zoe twirled the little straw in her drink. It was agony not to drain it and order another. But talking with John was helping distract her and she had succeeded in pushing thoughts of Brayden from her mind. So far she wasn't doing the thing she often did where she tried to imagine what he'd look like if he were alive today.

"I love the hand gallops. The trick is to get going way

back, as soon as you can. People wait too long and then they're already looking at the jump and it's too late. They chicken out because they're already looking for the distance. If you establish your pace first, it all falls into place."

"That's good advice."

"You should try it next time."

"If there is a next time. I'm pretty happy just doing the riding at home for now."

The conversation was easy between them, never forced. The longer they stayed at the pub, the more convinced she was she could make it through this night without getting wasted. But still, she'd have to go home alone, and that would be hard. Or would she?

There were none of the telltale signs, the come-ons she was used to. He wasn't casually bumping his knee against hers under the table, he wasn't leaning close to her, he hadn't put his hand on her back. He wasn't buying her drink after drink, or at the very least encouraging her to finish the one she had in front of her.

Still, he had stayed after Kirsten left, hadn't he? He clearly enjoyed her company. But was he attracted to her?

He paid the tab, insisting that it was the least he could do since he couldn't pay her to ride Gidget.

"What are you up to now?" she said as they readied to leave.

"Now?" He furrowed his brow. "Oh, like go out somewhere else or something? I'm really lame. I thought maybe you'd already figured that out about me. I'm just going home and going to bed."

"Bed is good." God, she was bad at being the one to come on to somebody. It always happened naturally, or the guy made it plain and clear what he wanted. "I haven't been sleeping that well, actually," Zoe continued. "I'd be up for coming over to your place and, I don't know, hanging out more."

He shook his head. "Nah, I don't think so. Not tonight."

A flat out refusal. He had no interest in her.

It stung.

The first thing that shot through her mind was that maybe he was gay after all. He could still be in the closet. There had to be some explanation for why he didn't want to sleep with her.

They briskly said good-bye, as if both of them wanted to be out of the lingering awkwardness as soon as humanly possible. Now the whole night felt tainted, Zoe thought, as she drove home. Their warm, comfortable conversation barely mattered anymore. Her face flushed as she thought of him turning her down. *Bed is good.* Had she really said that? Maybe it was how bad she was at coming on to him? No, it had to be because he was gay.

Then the truth invaded her thoughts. He didn't want her because she was a slut. Because she'd slept with so many other guys. Because he knew that Donnie had abused her. She had fooled herself into thinking that somehow he didn't know about her history because he was a small-time player and not a permanent figure on the show circuit.

But even if you didn't go from show to show, you heard the gossip in the same way that she knew about the latest celebrity break-up from *US Magazine*. He knew all about her and he didn't want to have anything to do with her. She was good enough to show his horse but not to sleep with.

Fine, she thought, straightening her back against the interior of her car seat. She gripped the wheel tightly. *Fine.* She didn't want to sleep with him anyway. He was a nice guy, sure, but he wasn't at her level. He wasn't at the level of Morgan, who owned a whole goddamn major league baseball team.

It was good he hadn't reacted to her invitation, because from now on there would be nothing between them. It would be platonic and that was that. She would ride his horse and she would win on it. People would notice her again and pretty soon she'd have a real job back on the show circuit, hopefully far away from Bedford, New York.

Back in her crappy apartment, she ached inside. It was a terrible, lonely ache and she craved filling it with sex or booze or drugs. If she had been in a hotel room, she would have absolutely cracked open the mini bar and then made her way to the real bar and found a guy to sleep with. She could have gone on Tinder and seen if there was someone worth meeting up with nearby but it felt like too much effort.

Sometimes, Zoe was learning, self-control wasn't so much about actual intention but just access to resources. Her choices for self medicating limited, she turned on the TV too loud, hoping to quiet the voices in her own head that told her everything she did was shit, and no one could ever love her.

The TV was still on when she woke up in the morning. She may not have gotten wasted the night before or slept with a near stranger only due to lack of opportunity, but the fact that she was waking up sober and alone strengthened her resolve. Maybe she could do this recovery thing after all.

Chapter 12

ZOE LIVED UP to her promise to herself and focused on the training of Gidget with John. She stuck to her routine. She worked in the mornings at Narrow Lane, rode at Morada in the early afternoon, and then went over to ride Gidget in the late afternoons.

Zoe did a lot of flatwork with Gidget, or worked her over cavaletti and small gymnastics. John usually had a few interesting grids set up in his ring and it was perfect for getting Gidget's stride super adjustable and her mind dialed in too. For the handy portion of the derbies, she needed to be able to go from loping down a long line to turning on a dime to galloping a single oxer to trotting a log jump. Gidget had innate scope and style. What she needed to learn was adjustability and attentiveness.

The one thing Zoe soon learned Gidget didn't do well was trot jumps. The first time she trotted her over a vertical, the mare crow-hopped from much too far away and Zoe got completely left behind, like a fox-hunter in one of those classic hunt prints.

"What the hell was that?" Zoe said to John when she'd gathered herself back into the tack.

He was riding Cruz, the horse that Zoe agreed might make up to be a good eq horse, especially for a tall kid. He was nearly 17 hands and had an enormous step. John spent most of his time trying to get him adjustable. He didn't always jump the best with his front end—something else John was trying to work on.

"I don't know. Try it again. I guess I haven't done a lot of trot jumps with her."

This time Gidget broke into a canter a few strides away. Zoe pulled her up on the other side.

"I think we found her kryptonite," John said.

"Hello, trot jumps," Zoe said. "From now on all we'll be doing is trot jumps."

It was a bit of an exaggeration. Doing only trot jumps would likely give Gidget more of a complex about them. But she needed to get good at them if she was going to be a derby horse.

Zoe started trotting out of lines to begin with and that seemed to freak Gidget out less. Then she would head to a jump at the trot, bring her back to a near walk, and then push her forward again.

John rode different horses each day while Zoe rode Gidget. She began to feel like he was rotating them so she could see them and help him. As she became more comfortable, she would tell him what she was thinking—how a certain horse needed more impulsion or another needed to jump a lot of square oxers to get his front end better. She began to think how it must have been lonely for John to be riding all day at the farm by himself.

At first Zoe thought the fact that she had to cool Gidget down and put her away was annoying but she soon found she liked it. What did she have to race home to anyway? The TV and a bag of Doritos? She liked spending the time with Gidget and with John too.

She took to spending extra time grooming Gidget. She found the mare had a favorite spot about a third of the way down her mane. Zoe would rub it until Gidget would twist her nose in pleasure.

"Who loves me now?" Zoe would say to her. "Who's going to actually trot the trot jumps?"

They took turns using the wash stall and then grazed the horses alongside each other out front of the barn.

She and John talked about what they'd liked in school and what they hadn't. John had been a good student, taking honors classes and getting all As, which had made his decision to drop out of college for horses even harder for his parents to swallow.

"They pretty much freaked," he said. "I think they're still hoping I'm going to give up and go back to school so I can get a real job. I might have to if I don't sell a horse or two soon . . ."

Zoe hadn't liked much about school except for a few teachers she had who were zany and fun and actually seemed to care about the students. But she'd stopped going to real school after eighth grade and had gotten her diploma through tutoring services at the shows.

They had to talk a bit loudly because John couldn't let whatever horse he was grazing get too close to Gidget. Once or twice their conversation had gotten interesting and John had let his horse meander closer so they could talk more intimately. Of course this always ended with Gidget flattening her ears and threatening to kick or bite.

"Don't mess with the princess," Zoe told him.

Zoe had gotten used to Gidget's ornery personality, especially since it was mostly directed at other horses, not people. Gidget made nasty faces at Zoe from time to time but she'd never followed through on any of her threats and Zoe now kind of liked the fact that Gidget was a tough broad. The mare didn't take crap from anyone and Zoe admired that about her.

Zoe had also figured out that Gidget's favorite snack was bananas and glazed donuts so most days she brought her both.

"Don't you dare bite me," Zoe said to Gidget with affection when the mare made a face at her, or even went so far as to gnash her teeth.

John noticed Zoe becoming fond of the mare. "What's going on between you two?" he said. "Some sort of female-bonding-we-hate-men thing?"

"Gidget hates everyone, not just men," Zoe said. "She doesn't discriminate."

"What about you?" John asked.

"I don't think anyone has ever claimed I hate men," she said. Not wanting to go much further on the subject she added, "I love the fact that Gidget doesn't give a shit what anyone thinks about her. She doesn't apologize or feel badly for who she is. It's awesome."

"I'm glad you two are getting along."

"We are," Zoe said. "I can officially say she's one of the coolest horses I've ridden."

"That's saying something."

"Well, actually, in fairness, I've ridden a lot of crazy horses. Horses no trainer would let anyone else get on. And you should have seen the things my mother put me on when I was younger. It's a miracle I lived. I can't tell you how many times I got tossed off or crashed."

"And you kept riding?"

Zoe shrugged. "It didn't really bother me."

"I guess I can see why you and Gidget get along then."

Zoe had sworn she would keep it platonic with John and she did. But having a platonic relationship could not keep them from becoming close. Sometimes they skipped the ring work and went straight into the woods. There was a trail that led to a beautiful grassy field with perfect hills for training. A derby horse had to be fit and walking and trotting up the gentle slopes helped Gidget become aerobically fit at the same time that it built up her hind end.

Gidget was pretty brave in the woods. She didn't spook at every shadow or strangely-bent tree branch. Birds alighting from bushes or a squirrel rushing out from a pile of leaves didn't leave her in a jittering heap with her heart beating so hard Zoe could feel it through her legs against the mare's sides.

She did hate bugs, though, and just one deer fly could

make her crazy even with her requisite ear bonnet. She would swing her head to one side and then the other, anticipating one landing on her back.

Zoe nearly soaked her in fly spray before they went out and bought a fly whisk with a large plume of white hair from the nearby tack shop so she could vanquish any deer flies that dared land on the mare.

But once a deer fly had been in the general vicinity of Gidget, even if Zoe had then managed to smack it dead against the mare's neck, Gidget was a sweat-covered wreck. It was funny how such a large animal could be made nearly apoplectic by a small, albeit annoying, insect.

Once or twice a week, John brought Gidget over to Morada for Zoe to ride there. Then they could school her over the bright and imposing Morada jumps, and also jump the naturals on the grand prix field. On those days, Linda watched and helped and oftentimes so did Dakota.

Soon John asked Zoe to ride some of his other horses and the afternoons were spent training them together. He'd be setting the jumps or she would. Or they'd both be riding but would stop to watch each other and make suggestions.

"What was riding for Donnie like?" John asked.

Zoe felt heat rise up her back and neck. *Besides the fact that he verbally abused me at the ring and then physically abused me back at the barn*, she thought to herself? But that wasn't what he meant, hopefully.

"Donnie isn't exactly a rule-follower." She quickly added, "But he had nice horses and after my performance at the finals I wasn't exactly in high demand as a rider."

She worried he'd ask what happened, why she wasn't still riding for him.

"So you two broke up and that was it? He didn't want you riding his horses anymore?"

So he knew she'd been with Donnie. Not just riding for him, but *with him* with him. She told herself it didn't matter what he knew about whom she'd been with. She had no interest in him romantically. None at all. Well, that was what she told herself anyway.

"I left him," she said. "I couldn't be a part of the things he was doing anymore."

That was true. She couldn't be a part of getting beat up anymore.

"If you could work for anyone now, who would it be?" he asked.

"Honestly, I don't really know. I mean every trainer and barn has its plusses and minuses. There are some really great trainers but I don't know that they'd have the horses I'd want."

"Like who?"

"Well, like Linda for one. I'd love to work for Linda permanently but she doesn't have horses for me to show."

"Okay, another question. What one horse would you want to show if you could pick?"

"Present day horse or past horse?"

"Both," I guess.

"Past horse, Rox Dene. Present horse, hmmm, I guess Three Wishes. That horse is freaking amazing," Zoe said.

"Good choice."

"How about you?"

"Past horse . . . I guess I would have liked to get a shot at the eq finals on a horse like Clearway or Helio Rouge. Hell, even just on a horse that wasn't dead green and had been to Indoors before. Today . . . I'd have to say Rothchild. That horse looks like so much fun. He's just such a scrappy trier. I'd like to think if I were a horse I'd be Rothchild."

"If I were a horse, I don't know who I'd be."

Zoe laughed, thinking of the qualities that would make a horse like her. The horse would have to be pretty and a little crazy and make terrible decisions. "I'd like to be like Gidget. A suffer-no-fools kinda girl."

"Gidget's lucky she's a horse," John said. "I'm not sure her temperament would get her very far in life if she was a human."

"No," Zoe said. "It probably wouldn't."

Chapter 13

THE FEW WEEKS gearing up to the spring show season ticked along with schooling Gidget, helping John with his other horses, and riding for Linda. Soon it was the week of the first Old Salem shows.

John often took a horse or two to Old Salem. The A show at the gorgeous farm Paul Newman had once owned was right in his backyard.

Zoe was going to do Gidget in the high performance workings and if that went well the first week, she'd do the derby week two. Zoe would also be helping Linda at Old Salem. Since the show was close she would be able to go back and forth between the home barns and the show, and also fit in her hours at Narrow Lane.

On Tuesday afternoon, she went over to John's to help pack up, even though he'd told her he'd handle all the details for the show.

"Please tell me you hired a groom and he's meeting us at the show," Zoe said half-jokingly as he stepped out of the feed room.

"Don't you wish," he said. "But you can relax. I know how to get a horse ready for the ring. So go ahead and get back in your car and I'll see you at the show."

"No, I'll help. What's left to do?" She didn't give him time to protest further and picked up a few buckets from the pile of equipment in the front of the feed room. "Are these going?"

"You don't have to," John said. "I've got it all under control."

"I know," she said.

She was actually happy to help John as much as he needed. Between helping him and riding for Linda, hopefully she'd be so busy she wouldn't be overcome with jealousy at seeing all her old friends showing all their nice horses.

Zoe followed behind the trailer. Pulling into the show grounds, she felt nearly weak with nerves and anxiety. She always felt a little excited flutter when she pulled into a show and she usually figured that was just a nice reminder of how much she still loved horse showing after all these years. But this heavy blanket of anxiety was something altogether different.

John parked temporarily to check the stall chart and Zoe got out to join him. There, in neat grids on the posted board, were all the farm names she knew so well. Autumn Ridge, West Hills, James Sharpe, Inc. And of course Donnie's farm. All those behemoths had blocks of stalls. She and John had to lean close and search for his two measly stalls, which were next to Morada Bay. Dakota's horses weren't coming over to the show till Thursday and Linda had told them to go ahead and share her grooming and feed stall.

Zoe said a silent prayer of thanks that Donnie wasn't in her tent, or near it for that matter.

They got back in their vehicles and she followed John again, past the first few tents with the big rigs with the grooms rushing up and down the ramps, and the few two-horse trailers belonging to the last remaining riders who trailered their own horses and did their own work.

She and John teamed up to set up the stall, the grooming stall, and get Gidget and Cruz settled. John went to the office and picked up the numbers.

"I'm putting the numbers in my main trunk, just so you know," John told her when he got back.

"Next week any time I ride her we need to have her number on her or else she can get disqualified from the derby."

"I didn't know that rule," John said. "I guess I don't know much about the rules for the international derbies, just the regular ones."

"Stick with me, kid," she said with a grin.

When it was time for her to ride, Zoe tried to steel herself. She had no choice but face all the people she hadn't seen since Florida. She told herself just to smile when she saw them and act like nothing had happened.

What else could she do? She wasn't the first person to ever go up in flames and leave the horse show world in disgrace for a period and then come back to it. She could either limp in feeling bad about herself or fake confidence. Faking confidence seemed like the right choice.

The first person she saw was the barn manager for a barn she used to catch-ride a lot of horses for.

"Hi-ya, Cindy," Zoe called out, deciding that making the first move would be best. *Don't let it be awkward. Give a bright and chipper hello. A hello that meant: I'm back and I'm doing so well. Look how healthy and well-adjusted I seem!* If she did this to enough people, by the end of the day most of the entire show world would have been informed that Zoe Tramell was back and God, did she seem good.

"Zoe," Cindy said, almost startling like she'd seen a ghost.

Zoe could tell Cindy was trying to decide if she should ask where she'd been or how she was doing.

Cindy settled on, "Great to see you. You look great."

"Thanks," Zoe said. "I *am* great!"

This was the way it went as she rode Gidget around the showgrounds. She chirped hellos to grooms, trainers, riders, the show manager who was out and about on his four-wheeler, and the show announcer who was walking from the announcer's booth to the bathroom. They all seemed genuinely glad to see her and Zoe began to think this was not going to be nearly as difficult as she had anticipated.

Maybe these people actually liked her! Maybe, in fact, they felt badly for her and blamed Donnie for everything, even the saddle stealing, which of course wasn't at all related to him but one could argue that the flow chart went: Donnie knocked her around—her self esteem plummeted—making her turn to drugs—and get involved with even worse people—(Étienne)—which in turn led to helping him steal saddles. The flowchart wasn't exactly accurate but if it made her sympathetic to them, all the better.

A few, like Cindy, commented on how good she looked, a vague reference to the hell she'd been through. Several asked whom she was riding for. "I'm helping Linda Maro and showing a horse for John Bradstreet," became her go-to line.

People nodded and said, "That's great," even though they probably had no idea who John was. A few brave ones asked. She simply told them he had a sales barn in Bedford. All true.

Maybe the truth *could* set you free because she felt pretty damn good about how this was all going. Except she wasn't quite ready for the truth to set her free with John just yet. She hoped no one mentioned the saddles or the drugs to him. It was bad enough that he knew she'd been sleeping with Donnie.

The grand hunter ring was open for hacking and Zoe took Gidget on a tour. She flatted her around, amongst the many trainers getting horses ready for clients. Some had draw reins on their mounts or elaborate bits. Others sat deep in the saddle, over-flexing their horses. A few breezed around in half-seat.

Zoe made sure to circle around the clusters of jump standards. Gidget seemed relaxed but attentive, the perfect combo for a hunter.

As she was coming out of the ring, Callie Vish was headed in.

Callie was a young professional, a few years older than Zoe. They'd partied together a few times on Sunday nights in Florida.

"Hey, girl, it's good to see you back in these parts!" Callie said genuinely.

"Thanks."

"Who's this?" she pointed her reins to Gidget.

"I got myself a new derby horse," Zoe said proudly.

"Really?" Callie gave Gidget a thorough once over. "Cute."

"You should see her jump."

"Cool." Callie widened her eyes. "Are you doing better? I was worried about you."

"I'm so much better."

"Oh, good," Callie said.

Zoe spotted John approaching on Cruz. He asked how Gidget was going and said he was going to flat Cruz in the jumper ring. Zoe walked Gidget around the grounds while he worked Cruz. Then they walked back to the barn together.

The start of the spring show season always felt like a kind of rebirth. And the flowers and green grass made Zoe feel hopeful that rebirth was possible for her too.

Nearly everyone she passed on the way back to the tent said hello to her. She let herself enjoy the way John was seeing her, as a near celebrity walking the red carpet again.

She noticed some of the women checking John out. Probably wondering if he was gay or straight, and if he was straight if Zoe was sleeping with him.

"You got a braider lined up?" she asked him.

"I braid."

"Really? Do you braid good?"

"I think so. This isn't exactly how you're used to doing a horse show, huh?"

"Not really," Zoe said. "But it's all good."

"Seriously?"

She gave him a big smile. "Seriously."

* * *

Zoe was grateful to be back at a horse show with a horse to ride. It wasn't the six or seven horses she was used to riding but it didn't matter. The routine and motion of the show was incredibly comforting. The way everything cycled along just like always. The hum of the barns as the grooms finished their last stalls and hoisted riders up onto their first mounts of the day. The smell of bacon drifting over from the food tent. The people coming in and out of the office, there to make a last minute entry change or file a medication report.

Closer to eight o'clock came the tinny barn calls by the in-gate crew, entreating riders in the first classes to get up to the ring. Then the formal announcement that the show was getting underway and the list of officiating judges. Even hearing the judges' familiar names was comforting, like hearing a name of a childhood pal. The same judges had scored Zoe so many times before, had judged her from her earliest days on the show circuit. They knew her well, had watched her grow up from pony kid to junior to now professional.

The high performance hunters went after the first and second years, of which there weren't a ton. After Gidget's stall was cleaned, John braided her up. Zoe had to admit John braided well. Maybe not quite as perfectly as the professional braiders but close enough.

Instead of getting more nervous as the class approached, Zoe felt emboldened. This was what she knew how to do. She knew how to find ten jumps. She knew how to make the space between those jumps look smooth and beautiful. She knew how to be subtle in her aids so the judge sat back in his or her chair, barely marking the card; instead just watching.

Inside the ring, she was confident and clever. She made good choices and knew how to make things come out right. It was outside the ring that her life tended to go haywire. It was outside the ring that she seemed to have the opposite of good intuition, always making the tragic choices.

Before she tacked up, she spent a few moments in the stall with Gidget. The mare sniffed her pockets, nibbling on the fabric of her jacket when she didn't find anything to her liking.

"I'll give you a banana after if you're good," she told her.

Gidget shook her head as if she was annoyed by this answer. Zoe turned to leave and Gidget reached out and nipped her arm, just hard enough to make it hurt, but not so hard as to break the skin.

"I thought you didn't bite," Zoe said with a little bit of an edge to her voice.

Gidget drew back quickly like she was expecting some sort of punishment, her ears flattened and her head down.

Zoe softened her voice. "Don't worry, girl. I'm not going to hurt you. I'm not that mad. It was a love bite, right? That's all."

Gidget still cowered in the corner. It was a pitiful sight. "Truce," Zoe said. She softly patted her neck. "Let's go show them what we can do."

More than ever it felt like she and Gidget were aligned in proving everyone wrong who had ever put them down or treated them badly.

John gave her a leg up and she rode up to the ring for the classes, with him following a few steps behind her. Gidget's neck looked beautiful, stretched out in front of Zoe with the line of tight braids. Since she was out of her stall, her ears were pricked forward and her expression was happy.

Zoe sat tall in the saddle, feeling the weight stretch down through her legs into her heels. Every step Gidget took affirmed her confidence.

The schooling area was full of riders warming up. Grooms held horses by the side of the ring. Trainers conversed with clients.

Zoe reveled in the familiarity of it all. This was where she belonged. These were her people. She took the mare up to the in-gate and positioned herself so she could look at the courses.

That's when she heard the unmistakable voice of Donnie behind her.

"Lock up your tack trunks, people," he said loud enough for everyone in the general vicinity of the in-gate, and probably the schooling area too, to hear. "Zoe Tramell's back in town."

Zoe felt all the air go out of her lungs. Leave it to Donnie to be the one person who could cut her to the core. The one person who would sharply remind her of where she'd come from and what she'd done.

For a short happy time, she'd thought she could move on from what had happened during circuit. She had thought that others were willing to let her move on.

Not Donnie.

He wanted to make her remember, and make everyone else remember too.

She racked her brain to think of a cutting comeback. Something she could say to neutralize the uncomfortable situation. She wasn't sure if she was imagining it but she swore she heard a few chuckles behind her.

She had nothing. No smart comeback.

Her throat had that fuzzy feeling when tears are building up.

John came to stand next to Zoe, facing her, his hand on Gidget's neck. "That guy's an asshole and if you want me to fight him I will."

She had been about to cry, but now she burst out laughing. The preposterous image of John fighting Donnie, here at the in-gate, flashed through her mind.

"You don't think I can take him down?" John pretended to look hurt. "Because I can. Right here, right now."

"He's not worth it," Zoe said, a few drops of moisture slipping from the corner of her eyes.

John made a fist and exaggerated a severe face. "You sure?"

"Yes, I'm sure, but thank you," she said.

She could have thrown her arms around him. She could have even kissed him. For saving her with a few joking words.

For making her see that Donnie wasn't worth it.

"When do you want to go?" John asked her.

"First," Zoe said.

Chapter 14

SOME RIDERS didn't like to go first but those were generally the juniors and the amateurs. The professionals usually didn't mind. There were certainly times when Zoe wouldn't have wanted to go first, like in a derby so she could see how the course rode, but there were only six in the high performance hunters, the courses were straightforward, and the longer she waited to go in the ring, the more time she'd have to get nervous.

The second years wrapped up and the jump crew hustled out to hike the jumps and rake in front of them. Zoe and John headed out to the schooling area. John commandeered one of the jumps; Donnie had the other.

Now he was using his physical presence to intimidate her. Earlier it would have worked. She might have fallen to pieces.

But not now.

Not with John on her side.

Let him be a prick, she thought to herself. *I'm not going to let him get to me.*

Alison Raynes was riding for Donnie now. She was a good rider, not amazing, but solidly good. She was in her mid-thirties and had bounced around from barn to barn since she'd been a junior. She was probably sleeping with Donnie too, although Zoe didn't know that for sure.

It was amazing Donnie got anyone to sleep with him but that was the horse show world for you. You could be crass, and not very attractive, and still get laid regularly. If more men knew what it was like they'd take up riding instead of golf.

"Where the hell did you come from?" Zoe heard him say to John. "East butt-fuck nowhere?"

"Bedford, New York," John answered flatly.

"You know about this girl?" he stabbed a finger in Zoe's direction where she was cantering Gidget around.

"You're acting like a dick," John said. "And we need to warm-up. So, let's just agree to not talk and both focus on our jobs."

"Do you know who I am?" Donnie said.

"I don't really care who you are," John replied.

Zoe was coming around the corner. She hadn't planned to jump quite yet but she decided the best thing to shut Donnie up was to get jumping so she cantered down to the low ramp oxer John had set up. It was either that or run Donnie over, which did sound appealing. She maneuvered a half-turn and John put the back rail up a hole so she could jump it the other way. Mercifully, Donnie shut the hell up for the rest of the warm up.

"She looks ready," John said after Zoe finished over a tall vertical.

"She feels good," Zoe agreed.

Donnie finished right after her and trailed her to the in-gate.

The ring sat empty. The course ready. Zoe just hoped the judge hadn't taken this moment to take a walk to the blue room.

"They ready for me, Kevin?" Zoe called out to the in-gate guy as John quickly wiped off her boots and Gidget's mouth, and slapped on the hoof oil.

"Yup, head on in."

John had barely finished taking off Gidget's tail wrap as Zoe nudged her into the ring. She had to pass by the judge's booth on her way to the first jump, a single coming home, and she smiled and said a polite hello.

Then she kicked Gidget into a canter and nailed the course. Not a distance one hair off. Not a jump that Gidget didn't show endless scope over.

Zoe came out of the ring acting calm and composed when all she could think in her head was, *take that, Donnie.* John looked a little shell-shocked, like maybe he couldn't believe that this was his horse or that a rider like Zoe was riding his horse.

"Wow," he said.

"She went well, huh?" Zoe said.

"Yeah," he said.

Her second round was just as breathtaking. She got the top call in both classes, beating out Donnie's horse. Leading the jog, having her name announced—*Zoe Tramell up for the ride on John Bradstreet's Girl Next Door*—being handed the blue ribbons, never felt so good.

Donnie glared at her as she came out of the ring, but didn't say anything besides a few mumbled swears.

"I think you've got a really nice horse on your hands," Zoe told John on the walk back to the tents.

"It wasn't *just* the horse," he said. "I thought you rode well at home but, well, I don't know, it's different in the ring. You've got this like, presence. It was pretty freaking awesome to be a part of, even if I'm a super small part of it."

"First of all, you're not a small part of it. You're a big part of it. What you said to Donnie Douchebag? You saved me."

John blew out a forced breath. "That guy's a total asshole."

Outside their stalls, Zoe hopped off, ran up the stirrups, and loosened the girth. John took the reins over Gidget's head. He was about to walk the mare into the aisle, when Zoe said, "What Donnie was saying . . . about the saddles. Did you know about all that already? Did you know that stuff about me?"

"I read something about it in *The Chronicle*, yeah, but I guess I don't know the whole thing."

"I'll tell you everything sometime, okay?" Zoe said.

"Only if you want to," he said.

Gidget won both over fences classes the next day and was third in the hack, making it quite the debut. Nearly immediately Zoe started fielding questions about her—where she'd come from, what had she done, was she for sale?

Zoe told John people were asking about her.

"For real?"

"For realsies," she said. She could tell he was grateful that the mare was getting some exposure. But soon after that, he wasn't happy with her at all. It started when he showed Cruz in the jumpers. Cruz was wild, running at the jumps, and seeming to not care the slightest if John took a hold of him.

"Looks like someone needs a little dental work," Zoe joked to John. "A little floating action."

"What are you talking about?" John said.

"I mean take him home and rip his teeth out over a few jumps," Zoe said. "Get him to listen to you."

"I wouldn't do that," John said, giving her a disapproving look.

"It's not like it's abuse or anything," she said in her defense.

"Depends on who you ask," John countered.

"You're acting like it's all terrible and I'm horrible for just saying the horse needs a bit of a school."

"Your idea of a bit of a school and mine appear to be different."

"That's how things are done at big barns," Zoe pointed out.

"I guess that's why I'm not a big barn."

"Okay," Zoe said. "Whatever. It's your horse."

John brought Gidget home and Linda trucked Dakota's horses in. It was their first time out since Florida and they were all fresh too. Zoe had to do some extra schooling sessions to get them quiet. The only exception, of course, was Midway, who was never not calm.

Zoe told Linda how John had been all natural horsemanship. "He acted all holier than thou when I was just saying the horse needed a good school." Zoe couldn't help but think about how John didn't know the first thing about what it took to win on the circuit.

Linda had Dakota ride Dudley for her first time out since Florida and let a working student for Hugo Fines ride Plato. Hugo was pretty much the top equitation trainer in the country, and one of the winningest trainers, period. His farm, Autumn Ridge, was a huge operation with multiple trainers and multiple billion-dollar clients. Dakota got good ribbons with Dudley and Plato went well for the boy too.

Midway ended up champion in the younger large juniors since some of the fancier horses were fresh too, spooking at a shadow or playing in the corner of the ring.

The following week, John brought Gidget back again, this time with the plan of doing the derby. She was champion again in the high performance working hunters and John and Zoe talked about going out to celebrate. Linda said she would go but, later in the day, she said she was much too tired and her back killed and she'd have to take a rain check.

The restaurant was quiet and intimate, with only fifteen tables. The food was artistic-looking and delicious. It was definitely a place people came on dates. "I'm sure the waiter thinks we're on a date," Zoe said to John out of nervousness. She hadn't thought she'd be here without Linda.

"Do you usually only date guys on the show circuit?" John asked.

"It's kind of hard not to," she said. "I don't meet many people who aren't show people. What about you? Do you have a girlfriend?"

He hadn't mentioned a girlfriend and there had been no

telltale signs of one (lock screen photos of the two of them, hair elastics, and other female paraphernalia in his car). This seemed like a good moment to find out. Even if she was keeping it platonic, she still wanted to know.

"No, not now. I was dating someone for a while but it didn't work out."

"Horse girl?"

He nodded. "We met in college before I dropped out. We rode on the team together."

"Is she still in horses?"

"No, she's taking a break. She's in law school in Boston."

"Got it. So was it the long distance thing that killed it?"

"Yeah, I guess so. We were well matched, I would say, but there wasn't ever, like, tons of passion."

Zoe rearranged her fork and knife. "She wasn't good in bed?"

John took a sip of his beer, looking like he was caught off guard. "I didn't say that exactly."

"It feels like that's what you meant."

"I just meant there wasn't much chemistry between us. I think we were just better off being friends. What about you? Boyfriend?"

"No, not now. I'm not usually very good at relationships."

"Why not?"

"I don't know. It's not that I don't want one. I guess I don't pick guys that make good boyfriends. Like Donnie. You must think I'm like the worst person for having been involved with him."

"I guess I just have to wonder why . . . like what was up with that?"

"I was working for him. We were winning a lot. That can be kind of intoxicating, I guess you'd say? I think I just got caught up in it all. One night it just sort of happened, and then, well, I guess this is where I tell you everything that happened . . ."

Zoe inhaled sharply and let it out. "Okay, I mean you probably know a lot of this already but Donnie treated me like shit, like really badly, abusively badly. But of course I didn't leave him. At the same time I got involved with this other guy, who worked for Arouet, you know the custom saddle place.

"He was into drugs—using and selling. I helped him get the gate numbers to farms and numbers to tack room locks and he stole the saddles. I never went with him or got any of the money."

Zoe realized she was avoiding taking responsibility—something she'd talked about with her counselor just last week.

"But I helped him do it by giving him the access so I was a participant in it. Finally, I went to the police and I turned him in. I got off with probation, court-ordered therapy, and community service—that's why I'm at Narrow Lane."

Zoe felt like she'd just got off her eighth ride of the day. Her arms and legs felt wobbly, even though she was sitting down. But she had said it. She had confessed everything. Well, everything except the part about her being bipolar. Maybe that would make what happened more understandable but she didn't want to tell him just yet. She was still coming to terms with the label herself.

"Wow," John said. "That's some crazy stuff."

"It's worse than you thought, right? Like now you don't want me to ride your horse? You're scared I'm going to steal your stuff?"

"Of course not," John said, but he looked away from her a little too quickly.

"I'm trying to do better now. To make better choices. I was in a really bad place back then and things are much better now. *I'm* much better now."

"I have something I should tell you," John said.

Zoe rubbed her hands together. "I hope it's juicy." She couldn't for the life of her imagine what kind of secret John had to reveal to her, unless he was gay after all, which would be a real shame. But nothing about him seemed gay and he'd just confessed to having a girlfriend, although the sex hadn't been great.

"You're gay," she blurted out.

John had been leaning in and he pulled back abruptly. "What? You think I'm gay? Do I seem gay to you?"

"I don't know, I just figured . . ."

"I'm not gay," John said. "Why does every guy who rides have to be accused of being gay? It's like if you're straight and you ride you have to spend half your life proving you're not gay."

"Maybe that's why most straight horse show guys sleep around all the time, to prove they're not gay. I'd never thought of that before. It's like to prove their virility." Zoe chanced a look at John. "So you're not gay?"

"No, I'm not."

"Then what is it?"

"I live at home. With my parents and my sister."

Zoe chuckled. "That's your big reveal? That you live at home?"

"Yup, that's it."

"So do most of our generation. If I could live at home, I would because I basically can't afford to have my own place, which is why it's totally crappy."

"I live there because it's affordable—I mean I haven't sold a horse since last fall and also because my parents need help with my sister—carrying her up the stairs sometimes, stuff like that."

Was John telling her because that was why he had put her off when she had come on to him the night they'd gone out for drinks? Even if he had wanted to, could he not take her home because home was *home*? Still, she had a place they could have gone to, and no guy she had ever known who was interested in sex let a lack of appropriate location stop him. But maybe that was just it, though. John wasn't like the other guys she had known.

For the first time since he'd turned her down, she had a little bit of hope again. Maybe John *was* the right guy for her.

Chapter 15

THE COURSE FOR the derby was open to hand-walk at noon on Saturday. Some riders had their grooms hand-walking their horses, especially if they had multiple mounts, but Zoe took Gidget on a tour herself, letting her sniff a few of the spookier jumps.

The jumps looked larger than any had in the hunter ring all week and also more solid. There was a wide green roll top and a jump made out of the round hay bales usually found in the middle of a huge field down south.

The only people who had watched Zoe pilot Gidget in the high performance hunters were the few trainers with horses competing against her. Now, however, the sidelines were full of trainers, riders, and owners. The announcer gave a quick run-down of how the derby worked in terms of the two rounds, the open numerical scoring with two judging panels, and the extra points awarded for jumping the four high options.

Zoe and John walked the course together, determining what strides to do in the bending lines and where, if anywhere, Gidget might decide to be spooky. Zoe said she felt good about planning to take all the high options. If Gidget started to unravel for any reason, she'd amend her plan and choose the lower jumps.

Zoe drew tenth in the order and felt very prepared as she walked into the schooling area to warm up. Everything felt like it was on target.

Until after her first jump when Gidget's fake tail fell out.

"You're losing parts," Alison Raynes called out with what Zoe was sure was a smirk.

Zoe pulled Gidget up and John collected the tail from where it had landed in the dirt.

The first rider waited at the in-gate and would be in the ring soon. She was junior rider, Jane Hewitt, a professional's kid. She was Dakota's age, one of the youngest riders in the derby, and her trainer was giving her a pep talk.

Zoe said to John, "I'm not sure we have time to put it back in."

"Should we just go without?" John asked.

"Without a fake tail?" Zoe had never found herself in this position before. All the horses she'd ridden before were expertly groomed and braided. "Maybe you should have had her professionally braided, at least for today," she said.

"I put the fake tail in fine yesterday and the day before and last week," John pointed out. "This happens to everyone sometimes."

"Fine, whatever," Zoe said as the first rider entered the ring. "Let's just go without it."

So one thing had gone wrong. It wasn't the end of the

world, Zoe told herself as they continued to warm up. Only it wasn't just that one thing.

Four jumps later, Gidget threw a shoe.

"Crap," Zoe said.

"Should we scratch?" John asked.

"Scratch?" Zoe said, astounded at how quick John was to bow out. "No, we just need to get the shoe tacked back on. We'll move down in the order."

She hopped off, instructing John to take Gidget over to the show farrier. She went to the in-gate to let Kevin know they needed to move down, probably to go last of the 36 entries.

She texted John to make sure he'd found the farrier and to let him know she'd wait by the ring.

As she waited she watched the rounds. It was interesting to see who was riding which horse, how the horses were going after Florida. Some horses thrived on showing at the same place all circuit, and looked nervous now that they were in a new setting. One horse ran out at the roll top and another stuck off the ground at the log pile.

Other horses looked reinvigorated by the change in scenery, relieved not to be pounding away in the same ring week after week.

Alison rode into the ring on one of Donnie's. She went straight to the canter, probably trying to conceal a slight lameness. She put in a good trip, except for one rough lead change. Donnie whooped like crazy and the scores came in on the higher side with the points added on for the high options. She took the lead in the class.

Zoe looked down at her phone. No text back from John. What was taking so long?

Everything okay? she typed. She would kill him if he found a way to draw this out so much that they couldn't go.

Yup, just not the speediest farrier I've ever met . . .

Zoe looked at the in-gate to see who was on deck. Cassidy Rancher was surrounded by what could only be described as an entourage. There was the trainer, the assistant trainer, the assistant-assistant trainer, two grooms, and a road manager with Cassidy's mother hovering nearby.

Cassidy motioned in the air with her pointer finger, going over her course by drawing an imaginary line from jump to jump.

The assistant-assistant trainer offered her a drink from an infuser water bottle. Cassidy waved her away.

Zoe watched, transfixed.

She had seen Cassidy ride plenty of times before. She'd even competed against her. But things were different now. Cassidy was the "it" girl of the show circuit. She was the prom queen, the MVP. She was the best junior rider in the country.

Cassidy knew it and so did everyone else. She had a long line of trainers and hangers-on. She had owners clamoring for her to ride their gorgeous horses. She had the luxury of telling no to half of the people who asked her to throw a leg over their mount.

Cassidy entered the ring and the buzz of conversations along the rail quieted. The spectators were expecting greatness, and wanted to be a part of that greatness, if even for a few moments. If only so they could go home to their barns and say they'd seen Cassidy Rancher ride and yes, she was as good as people said.

"Next on course from our junior division we have Cassidy Rancher riding her first of two mounts today. She's currently up on Lawless, a nine-year old Belgian-bred gelding owned by Hugo Fines and the Autumn Ridge Farm."

Cassidy rode brilliantly, making the high options seem effortless. Zoe felt more antsy about Gidget and the shoe, when really it was all because she wished she was Cassidy. It wasn't even that she wished she rode as well as her—Cassidy was maybe a hair better, but Zoe felt she was close in talent. It was Cassidy's position in life Zoe was jealous of.

Cassidy was still a junior, that blessed time where the world seemed limitless. Where your parents still paid the bills, or other people did. Where trainers let you stay with them and took you out to meals because you built their reputation. When people talked about how amazing you rode and how young you were, how poised in the saddle.

They even forgave your mistakes—riding or otherwise—chalking them up to youthful folly.

Once you graduated from the junior ranks, people automatically expected you to act professionally, to make all the right choices, to essentially grow up overnight. But just because you could no longer show in the junior divisions didn't mean you were a full-fledged mature adult.

Suddenly Zoe felt overcome by a burst of vindictiveness toward Cassidy. She imagined fast-forwarding a few years to when Cassidy herself aged out. It wouldn't all be so amazing then, would it? She wouldn't have trainers fawning all over her anymore.

She'd be just another talented rider in a sea of other talented riders trying to find good horses and eke out a living. Cassidy's life might seem perfect now but Zoe took glee in the fact that time would catch up with Cassidy Rancher too.

Cassidy finished her round and her entourage went crazy with the whooping. The two panels of judges handed out scores in the high nineties.

Cassidy gave her horse the obligatory pat even though Zoe knew she thought her scores were more a product of her, than the horse. It was probably true that if another rider had laid down the same trip on the same horse, the scores might have only reached the high 80s or low 90s. Those extra points were the Cassidy Rancher factor.

Zoe turned away from the ring, her jealousy making it impossible to watch anymore. She couldn't stand to see everyone fawn over Cassidy.

She spotted Linda and Dakota coming toward her and nearly wanted to run and hug them, utterly grateful for their presence.

"Where's Gidget?" Linda said.

"She threw a shoe. After she lost her fake tail. John's getting the shoe tacked back on."

"How was Cassidy?" Dakota asked.

"Perfect," Zoe said.

The class was nearly through by the time John hustled Gidget up to the ring.

"Are we in time?" he asked, slightly out of breath.

Linda tightened the girth and pulled down the stirrups while Zoe did up her chin strap and pulled on her gloves. "Barely." She was going to make a crack about self-sabotage but let it go, deciding to concentrate on the class.

"I'll tell Kevin you're getting ready," Dakota said.

As she warmed up Zoe worried what would go wrong next. First, the tail. Then the shoe. Bad things ran in threes, didn't they? She told herself she was being ridiculous but her mind flitted between what might go wrong in the ring, and Cassidy Rancher and how lucky that girl was to be so young and good, and why John seemed to be happy underachieving.

As she rode up to the in-gate and saw the course she was about to ride, Zoe's mind cleared. Thankfully the only thing she was soon thinking about were the jumps and her horse.

Gidget was maybe the tiniest bit spooky over the new jumps but it only made her jump better. Zoe could feel her skying over the fences, even the high options.

She finished to John and Linda's whoops and scores in the low nineties.

The handy round didn't have a trot jump, which seemed like a gift from the horse show gods. Instead there were several roll backs, inside turns, and a hand gallop. They came back in reverse order of their first round scores, which meant Zoe came back third to last. Alison sat between Zoe and Cassidy on one of Donnie's horses—not the one with the late change but his second entry, which had gone better.

Gidget was slick through all the inside turns and roll backs and she jumped crazy good. She didn't touch a rail, not even a tiny rub. Zoe really pressed her for the hand gallop too.

Once out of the ring, she slid off Gidget and gave her a hearty pat while John ran up her stirrups.

"See what we can do together?" she said to the mare.

She watched Cassidy's handy round from the in-gate, pretending to not care as much as she did. In her head, she wished for Cassidy to reveal her human side and flub a distance.

But her round was flawless and Zoe knew before the whooping had died off and the scores had come in that she wouldn't beat Cassidy. Not today. The scores confirmed it. Cassidy had won with Zoe in second.

"Not bad for your first derby with her, " Linda said as the ringmaster prepared for the awards ceremony and nearby a horde of people congratulated Cassidy, gushing over how well she'd ridden.

"No kidding," John said.

Both of them noticed her looking a little disappointed.

"You would have liked to beat Donnie," Linda said.

"And Cassidy," Zoe admitted.

"So basically you're not happy unless you win?" Dakota said.

"I'm happy, but yeah, I always want to win." She glanced meaningfully at John. "That's the way it's supposed to be. You're not supposed to want to come in second."

Chapter 16

ZOE WAS GLAD that Narrow Lane wasn't closed on Mondays like most horse show barns. Lessons at Narrow Lane went on as usual. Molly rode and Zoe was so glad to see her. John had brought Molly Gidget's ribbons and Molly told Zoe she'd hung them up in her room.

Zoe stayed longer at Narrow Lane than she was required to and still didn't want to go home to her grim apartment. Instead she popped over to Morada Bay. Linda shouldn't have been there on her day off but Zoe had the feeling she might be and she was right. Linda was in the office, working on the computer.

"Hey, girl," Zoe said as she came into the office.

"I'm so glad you're here," Linda said. "I was going to text you to see if you could come by."

"What's up?" Zoe said, looking concerned. She couldn't imagine what was so time sensitive. Had Linda hired someone else? Did she not need Zoe anymore?

"I went for my MRI this morning."

"Oh, right, shit." Zoe felt like a jerk for not having re-membered and for not having asked right away, or better yet, texted her earlier. "I totally forgot. I'm sorry. I don't know where my brain is. What did they say? Do you get the results right away?"

"I don't even know because I didn't actually have the MRI."

"What? Why not?"

"Because one of the questions on the form they made me fill out beforehand asks whether you might be pregnant . . ."

Zoe's hand flew up to her mouth. "Oh no, you might be pregnant?"

"No, I *am* pregnant," Linda said. "I thought there was a chance I might be since I was late so I told the nurse at the MRI place and she said I shouldn't have the MRI till I go get a pregnancy test just to make sure so she sent me to the lab at the hospital and I had the blood test and, I'm pregnant."

For Zoe, pregnancy always loomed, a probable conse-quence of her reckless lifestyle. It was why she'd gone on the pill back when she was sixteen but too many times she forgot to take it. She had been late herself a few times and had stressed endlessly about whether she might have to get an abortion.

So far, somewhat miraculously given her sexual history, she'd managed to avoid getting knocked up.

"You don't look like I'm expecting you to look." Zoe ex-pected Linda to be anguished but her face was placid.

Linda finally broke into a smile. "I'm happy. I'm very happy."

Zoe shook her head like she'd missed something big. "Wait, you're not married, you just started dating Eamon, and you're happy? It is his baby, right?"

"Yes, it's his." Linda repositioned the sunglasses she always wore on top of her head. "I'm thirty-six. I'm single. And I'm a horse trainer. These are like the three worst things you can be if you ever want to have a family. I live a nomadic lifestyle in a world where the men get to screw around with pretty girls ten or twenty or even *thirty* years their junior and no one thinks anything of it. I've always wanted to have kids, or at least one kid. I hadn't really given up. I'd sort of told myself that it was still possible till I was forty at least. But it didn't look like it was about to happen anytime soon. And now I'm actually pregnant and I'm pretty sure I'm in love with Eamon."

"Have you told him yet?"

"About which part? The baby or the might-be-in-love-with-him?"

"The baby."

Linda looked concerned for the first time that day. "Not yet."

"He's Irish, though," Zoe said, rushing to reassure her. "They love kids and family. It's like super important to them."

"I know, that's what I'm praying for. But, honestly, if he doesn't want this baby, I don't think I care. I'm having it myself."

"Good for you. You totally should," Zoe said, even though she had no idea what she was talking about.

Zoe reflected for a moment on the fact that Linda had chosen to share her news with her when she didn't know the first thing about having kids, or even having a healthy relationship. She was touched that Linda had confided in her, even if it was just because she knew she wouldn't be the type to judge her.

"When are you going to tell him?" It seemed like the next logical question.

"I don't know. I think I'll wait till I see him in person again. I guess at HITS. Don't you think that sounds good? I mean better than doing it over the phone?"

"Definitely. In person is always better for big news. You don't want to text, like, *guess what? You're my baby daddy!*"

She and Linda burst out in laughter. "I can't believe you're pregnant," Zoe said. "What about your back? Can you still have the MRI?"

"I set up an appointment with my OBGYN for Wednesday. I'm going to ask her."

"Are you going to tell the Pearces?"

"At some point. Not yet. I'm only eight weeks pregnant." Linda leaned back in her chair and beamed. "I'm going to have a baby!"

"Yeah!" Zoe squealed. "Let's go buy a pony!"

* * *

Only Linda chickened out and couldn't bring herself to tell Eamon at HITS.

"It's still really early," she told Zoe. "Maybe I'll just wait a few more weeks. Just to make sure it sticks, you know?"

John brought Gidget to HITS, since he could drive back and forth. It was over an hour drive and Zoe stayed at the show over the weekend so she wouldn't have to get up insanely early to help Linda.

Gidget ruled the high performance hunters again. The derby was a national class, which meant less prize money, smaller jumps, and not as many big name horses entered. But Zoe hoped it would have a trot jump in the handy because it would be a good way to try the trot jump at a show. Gidget had been getting better at trot jumps at home but she still tended to raise her head and tense up on the approach.

Her first round in the derby was great and she led the class going into the handy, which did have a trot jump. It was made of birch rails with lots of greenery on the sides. Zoe tried to calmly channel the mare between her hands and leg on the approach. It was hard because if she was too forceful and used too much leg Gidget would likely break into a canter step before the jump. But if she gave her too soft a ride, she might stick off the ground.

It was all about reading tiny signals in a fraction of seconds and responding appropriately. As Gidget saw the birch rails, her head came up and her body tensed. Zoe tried to comfort her with her leg but keep her feel of her mouth so she wasn't abandoning her. She thought she had pulled it off until at the last moment Gidget stuck off the ground. Zoe didn't get left but it wasn't pretty—that much she knew.

She recovered and finished the course well, but the damage was done. She had slipped to fifth place. Fifth place in a national class was just not good enough.

Back at the barn after the class, Zoe told John she thought they needed to work her in draw reins over tiny trot jumps. "I know you're not going to like this," she prefaced her suggestion with. She knew how he'd reacted to her suggesting he try to teach Cruz a lesson about not running through his hand.

He shook his head the moment he heard the word *draw*. "No."

"She puts her head up and we need to get her to learn to relax and keep her head down and just pop over the jump. I'm not talking about jumping a meter twenty with draw reins on. I'm just talking about tiny, tiny jumps, like cross-rail height."

"No," he said again.

"Okay, so what do you suggest?" Zoe crossed her arms.

"We just keep working with her the way we have been."

"We don't have time to keep doing it like that and there's no sense showing her in the derbies if she can't win them because she won't trot the trot jump."

"This is what I hate about the show circuit," John said. "Everything's a quick fix."

"I'm not suggesting anything cruel or illegal. But you said yourself when I first met you that she's a derby horse and that's exactly what she is. If you keep playing around with her in the high performance hunters and not showing her in the derbies while you take forever to fix the trot jump issue people are going to decide there's a reason why you're not doing the derbies and then you'll be stuck with a derby horse not showing in the derbies that no one will buy. I seem to recall you said you needed to sell some horses?"

John gave a reluctant nod.

"You need to trust me here," Zoe said. "There's no use taking her to Fairfield and Lake Placid if she can't jump a trot jump and it's a crime to leave a horse this good home."

"Who said anything about Fairfield and Lake Placid?"

"If we go along with Linda's schedule and do Fairfield, Lake Placid, and Vermont, that'll give her at least four more derbies before Derby Finals."

"Whoa, slow down. Derby Finals?" John said. "Don't you have to qualify for Derby Finals?"

But Zoe wouldn't slow down. She thought maybe if she talked fast John would give in and have to go with her plans. "She qualified at Old Salem. You want to sell your horses, you need to go to big shows. You could totally get Cruz and Dibs sold this summer if you take them and show them."

"I'm not sure they're ready for a show like Lake Placid," John said, putting her off.

"You have this idea that all the big shows are like amazing and every horse that walks in the ring is perfectly broke and gorgeous. You need to sit by the ring and watch some of the lower divisions. There's a lot of trash blowing around those rings."

"So you're saying my horses are trash?" he said playfully.

"No, I wouldn't ride your horses, or suggest we go, if your horses were trash. I think you have nicer, better-broke horses than *you* think you do. But I also think you have some ridiculous assumptions of what the big shows are like. There are so many horses and riders that suck there. That's why your nice horses would sell in a minute." Zoe hesitated.

"Well, I mean, with me to help broker them. It *is* who you know after all."

John smiled. "So you want a commission?"

"Actually, I don't really care, although I am broke. But I'm not angling for a commission."

"No, you'd deserve it. I should be paying you for all the riding you're doing for me, and the help you're giving me."

"I'm not looking for money," Zoe said. "That's not why I want you to take your horses. I want you to take them because I think your horses belong there. I guess I thought that's what you've been aiming for? I thought it was what you wanted."

"It is," John said.

"Good, then let's go." To her it was simple.

"I can't be away that long," John said. "I'm supposed to be taking care of the farm and who would ride the horses I left at home?"

"We could find someone local to ride the horses and so the grass at the farm grows a little longer while you're gone."

"I'd have to pay someone to ride them and do all the barn work I do. Feeding, night check."

"Which would be worth it when you sell a horse." Zoe hoped she wasn't promising something she couldn't deliver. But she had to get Gidget better at trot jumps and then she had to get to those shows. "I guess you could also just send Gidget with me and Linda."

"I want to go," John said. "It's not that I don't want to . . . It's my parents and Molly. It's hard to get her upstairs to her bedroom. Then you have to get her back down again in the morning . . ."

Zoe felt like an ass again. Of course he couldn't just take off and leave them. But if he couldn't go to the shows how was he ever going to make a living selling horses?

"I'm sorry. I didn't think of that. So let me take her then."

"Let me think about it," John said.

"See, you totally don't trust me with your horses." She remembered how John had looked at her the night she'd told him about Donnie and the stealing.

"It's not that. I just, I need to think about it. About going to those shows. But I feel like somehow you got me off the topic of draw reins."

"Because we already decided she needs to do trot jumps in draw reins and you're okay with it because you totally trust my judgment."

John smiled like he knew he'd been beat. "Fine, we can try it."

* * *

Of course John didn't even own a pair of draw reins. But Zoe found a pair in her car, buried beneath a lunge line, several bits, and a few gloves with holes at the ends of the fingers.

She rode her on the flat and over poles for several days, keeping the draw reins loose. Then she moved onto cavaletti and small jumps. She cantered them first so Gidget could get used to the idea of how they felt when she wasn't adding the stress of the trot jump.

John watched and seemed to approve.

"See, I'm not tying her nose to her chest," Zoe pointed out.

"Yet," John joked.

When she moved to trot jumps, the draw reins definitely helped. They subtly supported what Zoe was trying to achieve. When she turned the corner Zoe would feel Gidget begin to raise up her head and withers and then Zoe would put her leg on while taking a feel on her mouth and with the slight addition of the draw reins Gidget began to stop resisting and accepted keeping her frame. She started to get some good trot jumps where Gidget relaxed and used her back.

"Draw reins are okay in certain instances for certain riders," Zoe said. "Riders that know what they're doing. Are you convinced yet?"

"Getting there," John admitted. "Oh yeah—" He ran a hand through his hair, looking slightly uncomfortable. "My parents would really love you to come to dinner."

"Me?" Zoe had never been the type of girl parents invited over for dinner. She and John weren't dating, but she wasn't even the type of girl *friends'* parents invited for dinner. She was the type of girl parents warned their kids against hanging around with.

"They know how you've been helping me with Gidget and how much Molly likes you."

"Really? They want me to come over?" Zoe said again.

"Yes. You. Over. Dinner." John made a face. "How hard is this? Will you come?"

"I'll come," Zoe said. "Of course I'll come. When?"

"I thought maybe after Devon? How about Tuesday? Seven o'clock?"

Zoe was going to Devon for junior weekend to help Linda. Linda's back was a little better but she didn't want to do too much and hurt it again, especially now that she was pregnant. It would be the first time since Zoe was nine or ten that she hadn't shown at Devon. She'd only be preparing Dakota's horses. But at least she'd be there.

"That works." It wasn't as if she ever had plans.

"Great," John said. "I'm glad that's settled."

Chapter 17

ZOE OBSESSED ABOUT what to wear to John's. She should look nice but not sexy-nice. Definitely not sexy-nice. She wished to God she had a preppy little sundress—the kind that Julia and Bennett had closets full of. Hannah probably had a bunch of those kind of dresses too.

It was five after six and shopping wasn't an option. She had to go with something in her closet. She sent Hannah two options and Hannah picked a cute skirt that Zoe had bought at the J.Crew outlet in Vermont the previous summer and a tank with a sheer blouse over it and tied at the waist.

She checked herself in the mirror one more time before leaving. She had gotten a pretty bad sunburn at Devon. One of the days she'd been out in the sun for hours helping Linda school Dakota and standing at the in-gate when she went in the ring. Usually Zoe had a riding helmet on—she wasn't used to spending so much time in the sun without her helmet on and she'd fried her nose and forehead. Now, they still looked a little painful.

Why was she so nervous about going to his house? She wasn't dating him; it didn't matter if his parents liked her. Of course she wanted them to think that John continuing to partner with her professionally was a good idea but all that required was that she was mildly polite and no huge skeletons appeared from her past.

Their house was a small Cape. Cute and well tended with a little hedge surrounding the front lawn. They had one of those novelty mailboxes shaped like a dog, with a head and legs and a tail. A Golden Retriever to be exact. Judging by the size of their house, Zoe could understand why John had never had a competitive eq horse or been able to ride with a big name trainer. Their whole house could fit inside the kitchens of many riders on the circuit.

A real life golden retriever met her at the screen door.

"Hi, there."

John put a hand on the dog's collar and pushed open the screen door. "Come on in. This is Sutter. He's Harry's nemesis. Sutter gets his own mailbox and Harry gets nada."

Zoe spent a few moments giving Sutter a bit of attention. He was a beautiful dog with a lighter colored coat.

"I see you met the welcome wagon," Joanne said, joining them in the small entryway.

"Hi," Zoe said. "Thanks for having me."

Joanne looked a little less heroic outside of the barn, a little more like an average mom. Zoe noticed wrinkles at the corners of her eyes that hadn't been as apparent in the dim light of the indoor.

In the kitchen Zoe met John's dad. He had a full beard

and stood at the stove in an apron. Zoe looked around the kitchen at the framed children's artwork on the walls and the many family photographs stuck with magnets onto the fridge. It wasn't a gleaming stainless steel fridge, just a simple white one, and Zoe found the fridge with all its photos oddly comforting, like it was almost another member of the family.

There was a colorful kitchen mat on the floor at the sink—a bright pattern of intersecting oranges and cherries. A bunch of bananas hung on one of those banana hangers on the counter, next to a coffee maker. All hallmarks of a normal family life—the kind Zoe had never had.

"Dan's the cook in the family," Joanne said.

Zoe was relieved that Joanne wasn't a domestic goddess, in addition to being an amazing mother to a girl with a disability.

"I don't cook anything fancy," Dan said. "But I do cook."

"I'm not like a foodie or anything," Zoe said. "Give me a good burger and I'm a happy girl."

"Perfect," Dan said.

"Molly's watching TV," John said. "She can't wait to see you."

Zoe wondered why Molly hadn't met her at the door and then felt dumb when she realized Molly couldn't just walk from room to room on her own.

Zoe followed John to the family room where Sutter sat at Molly's feet. Harry lay sprawled out on a dog bed in the corner. He didn't lift his head; only barely opened his eyes.

"Hi, Molly," Zoe said.

Molly looked uncharacteristically shy. Zoe noticed the braces on her legs. She didn't wear them when she rode.

"Hi," Molly said weakly.

Everything about John's house was warm and welcoming and the family room was no exception. The plump couch had a blue and green plaid blanket over it, and a shelving unit held knick-knacks and books. Someone's fleece jacket was thrown over the arm of a chair and a mug sat on the coffee table. The house told of a regular, comfortable family life—of four people who loved each other dearly. It made Zoe never want to leave. This was the house she wished she'd grown up in.

"I really like your dog," Zoe whispered, holding up her hand to her mouth, pretending to try to exclude John, "Don't tell your brother but I think I like him better than Harry."

"We all do," Molly said.

"Wait a second," John said. "I do not love Sutter more than Harry. Harry may be in the twilight of his life and not be able to be all perky and cute like Sutter but I love that old dog." John got up and went to pat Harry. Harry closed his eyes and emitted a groan.

"How'd he get the name Sutter?" Zoe asked.

"From a movie," Molly said.

"Wait, Sutter from *The Spectacular Now*?"

Molly's face brightened and her shyness slipped away. "You know it?"

"Know it? It's like my all time favorite." Zoe turned to John. "You've seen it?"

"Yeah, it's a good one," John said.

"The part after the car wreck . . . when she asks if he's okay? Oh my God, that part kills me every time." Zoe held a hand to her chest.

"And what about when the store owner tells Sutter if he

was his dad he'd lecture him and Sutter says if he was his dad—" Molly said.

Zoe stepped in, "He wouldn't have to. One of the best movies. And I love the name Sutter. Great choice for your dog."

Of course Zoe couldn't help but think how Sutter was also McNair's last name, the grand prix rider Hannah had ill advisedly slept with.

"Thanks," Molly said.

Dinner was pork chops with a salad. "It's not a burger . . ." Dan said as they all sat down in the dining room.

"I love pork chops," Zoe said.

"Good," Dan replied, offering her a genuine smile.

Zoe noticed that Molly's pork chop had already been cut into tiny pieces. It was hard not to watch Molly work at piercing each piece with her fork and maneuvering it to her mouth. The tiny details of life Zoe took for granted were all challenges for her.

Joanne asked how Devon went. Zoe was somewhat surprised Joanne knew she had gone.

"Good, Dakota got ribbons in the eq and the hunters and she actually won a low junior jumper class." She turned to John. "Did you ever show at Devon?"

He shook his head and she wished she hadn't asked. She should have known he hadn't ever gone.

"You were best child rider there a few times, right?" he said. She couldn't tell if he was trying to show her off in front of his parents.

"Only once," Zoe said.

"Zoe, we are so happy you've been helping John with the horses," Joanne said.

Zoe wiped her mouth. "Me too." She glanced at Dan. "This is delicious, by the way."

"John's such a good rider, well, at least *we* think so," Joanne continued. "But it always seemed so hard to break through to the top level. John says you've done it all . . . won at the best shows. How did you find your way to the top like that?"

"I kind of grew up on the circuit," Zoe said. "My mom had a barn and it's like the only thing I've ever known."

"Do you love it like Johnny?"

Johnny. That was too cute. Zoe looked over at him. He made a face back at her.

"I do love it. I can't imagine doing anything else."

"But you love showing more than I do," John said. "I mean you really *love* being in the ring."

Zoe swallowed a bite of salad. "I guess I do. I'm not sure what that says about me really. That I'm a show-off or a diva or something?" She wished she hadn't used the word diva. John's parents probably thought all show circuit riders were total divas.

"Someone has to want to be the lead in the school musical," Dan said. "I'm not sure there's anything wrong with that."

"I guess in that scenario I'd be one of the people working on the set?" John said.

"Or the director," Joanne put in. "Did you go to college?"

"I'm only nineteen," Zoe said. "And, no. I didn't." She

looked down at her plate. Surely his family would think less of her for not having even tried college.

"She always knew what she wanted to do with her life," John said.

He was clearly trying to help her out and maybe defend his own choice a little too.

"Zoe likes *The Spectacular Now*," Molly said, a little out of nowhere.

"I do, I love that movie," Zoe said, happy for the change in subject. "I'm a big movie fan in general. I love the totally sappy romantic ones."

"That's where Sutter's name came from," Joanne said.

Zoe smiled. "That's what Molly said."

Joanne passed the bread basket over to Zoe. "We watch a lot of movies. I mean just here in the house. If you like movies, you should join us sometime."

"What about tonight?" Molly said.

"We all have to get up for work tomorrow," Dan said. "And you have school."

"Molly goes to an alternative school program," Joanne explained.

"John's told me about it. It sounds great."

"It is, right, Molly?" Joanne said.

"I like it a lot. Not as good as watching movies, though."

"I'd love to come back and watch a movie sometime," Zoe said.

"Maybe this weekend?" Molly asked.

"That'd be great for me."

Zoe helped do the dishes. She tried to do a good job and not bang plates on the sink or drop silverware on the floor.

She didn't have much experience in the kitchen, cooking or cleaning, but rinsing dishes and sticking them in a dishwasher couldn't be all that much harder than cleaning tack.

"Just load them in the dishwasher," Joanne said when she caught Zoe furiously scrubbing a plate like it was a snaffle with crud on it. "It'll get all the hard stuff off."

"Okay." Zoe finished loading up the dishwasher. Was she supposed to turn it on? Joanne must have seen her looking at the unit. "We'll turn it on later. It's not the quietest machine."

Zoe dried her hands on a dishtowel and rehung it on its hook. She went to the bathroom to make sure soap hadn't floated up into her hair, or something embarrassing like that.

Joanne caught Zoe as she was coming out of the bathroom. She seemed to be waiting for her, hoping to get her alone. "Thank you for helping Johnny out."

Zoe checked nearby for John before she spoke. The house seemed so small that you could be in any room and someone would overhear you. "Oh my God, he's helping me just as much. Linda doesn't really have horses I can show and, well, as John said, I kind of like being in the ring."

"But you took a chance on him. I know he's not at the same level as you . . . we couldn't afford to send him to a big barn. I never really thought he'd stick with this and do it for a living. I guess if we'd known he'd choose this as his profession maybe we would have tried harder to somehow get him on the A circuit. Who knew he would love it this much?"

"He's got a great eye for a horse. He's a good rider too."

She lowered her voice. "You think he can make a living doing what he's doing? Selling horses?"

"Plenty of people do. I mean, it's not like you're going to

make millions and I'm not going to say the lifestyle is super cushy, but people do make a living out of it."

"I want him to do what he loves . . ." she said. "But I also want him to be able to have a decent life doing it. So far the money's going out and not much has come in. How long does it usually take to sell a horse?"

"Totally depends on the horse and so many other factors really."

"Well, I just appreciate you helping him."

"Really, he's helping me just as much."

"Then let's just say I'm glad you two found each other." She looked at Zoe with what seemed like almost a twinkle in her eye. Did she think they were together? Hadn't John made it clear that they weren't?

"There is one thing," Zoe said. "To sell horses you really have to go to some away shows. Did John say anything about Lake Placid?"

Joanne shook her head.

"He thinks he can't go because you guys need him too much. And if you do, then I totally understand that, but what you just said about wanting to support his career more . . ."

"We can definitely manage. Johnny's such a good boy. He needs to put himself first more often but that doesn't come naturally to him, I guess."

"I hope you don't think I'm trying to take him away from your family," Zoe said.

"No," Joanne said. "I appreciate you telling me."

Zoe went back into the family room, hoping to find John there. She asked Molly where he'd gone.

"He's taking the garbage out."

Zoe spotted him through the window, opening the barrel and throwing the trash bag in. She went out the screen door as he was coming back in.

"Trying to make a run for it?" he said.

"No, I was coming to see if you needed any help."

He brushed his hands together. "All set. Was this bearable?"

"I never want to leave, actually."

He looked at her funny. "Seriously?"

"Seriously. I love your family. It's like the family I've always wanted."

"Okay," he said, still regarding her with a bit of a perplexed expression. "I saw my mom corner you before I went out. Did she tell you how she wishes I'd give up horses and go back to college?"

"No, she said she wishes she'd supported your riding more when you were a junior. If she'd known that you were going to do it for a living, she might have tried harder to get you riding with someone more big-time."

"Really?"

"Yeah, that's what she said."

"I don't want her to feel badly," he said. "She and my dad have done so much for me and Molly."

"I guess good parents always wish they could do more for their kids," Zoe said, although she really didn't know the first thing about that personally. Her mother barely ever called her and when she did it was to get a horse sold. When everything had happened in Florida, her response was, "Do you know what this could do to my business? Who's gonna want to buy a horse from me now?"

"I thought people feel parents today do *too* much for their kids," John pointed out.

"Maybe there's a balance. I mean look at Dakota's parents. They do all the *wrong* things for her. You wouldn't have wanted parents like that."

"No," John said. "I'm happy with the ones I got."

Zoe glanced back at the house. It was nearly dark outside and it looked so homey with the glow coming from the light inside. "Well, I guess I should go in and say good-bye."

"So you're not moving in permanently?" he said.

"Haha."

Zoe thanked Joanne and Dan and promised Molly they'd do a movie night soon. Joanne gave her a hug, squeezing her shoulders and not just errantly pressing against her.

Zoe walked slowly on her way out of the house, not wanting to go and leave the warmth and light there behind. It honestly might have been the nicest place she'd ever spent time.

She felt tears springing to her eyes. They were the kind of unexpected tears that hit you all of a sudden—a moment when you're not supposed to be crying but there you are, doing it. She tried to tuck her head down a little so John wouldn't notice but he did.

"Are you okay?"

"Yeah." She wiped away one teardrop that had slipped out. "I just had a really nice time, that's all."

"You can come back anytime. We'll do the movie night."

"I know," Zoe said, her voice still catching. "Just ignore me. Maybe I'm hormonal. It's like one of those crazy female moments." She hoped she could brush her tears off by making a joke. Usually guys forgave women if you just told them it was a female thing. It might negate years of effort by women trying to be treated equally but sometimes it had to be done.

She went to put her hand on the screen door and he put his hand over hers. "Are you okay to go home? I mean maybe you should just stay awhile longer?"

He set his gaze on her and they stood there, his hand on hers. There had to be something between them. It couldn't just be her imagination.

"I'm okay," she said. "I'll see you at the barn."

Chapter 18

ONE OF THE NEXT TIMES Zoe came to John's to ride she found him in the ring watching a kid trot around on Dibs. What must have been the kid's trainer was standing next to John.

Zoe didn't want to interrupt so she went into the barn and started grooming Gidget. A few minutes later, the three of them walked up to the barn.

"Thanks," the trainer said. "We'll be in touch."

Zoe had never seen the trainer before—she must have been a real local. She had full seat breeches on and really poorly-fitting dress boots, which meant she probably didn't do many big shows. The girl with her had one of those helmet covers in hot pink.

After they'd left, Zoe said, "How'd that go?"

"Let's see, a young, green hunter for a girl who started riding a year ago? Probably not the best match."

"Yikes," Zoe said.

"I should have just told them no the minute they got here.

I can't tell you how many tire-kickers I get. It's like people have nothing better to do than go around trying horses that are completely wrong for them. Some are so bad I just say no over the phone but you want to sell the horse . . . speaking of, I'm in for Lake Placid."

Zoe brightened. "Are you sure?"

"It's not like I'm going across the world. They'll call me if they need me and I'll go home."

"Okay," Zoe said. "Lake Placid here we come! Who do you want to take, besides Gidget?"

"I was thinking Gidget, Cruz, and Dibs. I already asked a girl I know from a local barn to ride the others. She isn't amazing but she can get them out and hack them around. And my stall guy's looking for extra work so he's more than happy to do the rest of the barn work. I can do Cruz in the jumpers and would you ride Dibs in the pre-greens?"

"I'd love to," Zoe said.

* * *

John lived up to his word and invited Zoe over to watch a movie with Molly. That movie led to another movie night and then another. In the weeks before they left for Lake Placid, Zoe happily found herself at the Bradstreets many times.

Some of the movies Molly had seen before but she wanted Zoe to see them, if she hadn't already, or to watch them with her. Zoe didn't mind seeing movies more than once. Even though she knew when the girl was going to be dumped by her fiancé, or when the boyfriend was going to die a tragic and untimely death, she still got weepy. John would roll his

eyes and poke fun at how sappy Molly and Zoe were but secretly it seemed like he kind of enjoyed the movies too.

Zoe loved those nights sitting on the couch with John and
Molly and Sutter on the floor at their feet and Harry snor-
ing/wheezing over in the corner.

Sometimes one of John's parents would watch with them,
or his dad would bring them bowls of popcorn. Zoe usually
sat in the middle of the couch and she was aware of how close
she was to John. Sometimes she thought she could feel him
looking at her when he should be looking at the TV.

She and John decided on a bit of whim to take Gidget to
do the Genesee Country Derby in Cooperstown. It wasn't a
typical derby—it was one of only a select number of stand-
alone USHJA derbies, meaning the rest of the horse show
wasn't rated. The setting was beautiful and bucolic, the
course set in a huge, rolling meadow and the jumps were all
old-hunt style—real stone walls, lots of brush, logs resting on
hay bales. Bright pink flowers sprouted from a trough carved
into one of the log jumps and an antique car stood in the
middle of the field.

It was a $35,000 class and some of the best derby riders
had shown up with their best derby horses. That included
Kendall Adams, who, like Zoe, had once been a top junior
rider. Her father was a big-time professional and her brother
rode too. Kendall concentrated on the hunters—her brother
had gone on to focus on the jumpers, riding for the team.

The family didn't have tons of money but they had all the
connections in the horse industry and Kendall's father had an
amazing eye for a horse, which meant he picked them up
wherever he could find them, and then put her on them.

Kendall was married now and had a six year-old son. Her husband wasn't a horse guy but it worked for them somehow. He tolerated the world he'd married into and in trade she didn't show every week, picking and choosing. Having her father as a full-time horseman helped her be able to take time off to spend with her husband and son.

Zoe saw Kendall hacking her best horse, Veracity, around the outside of the meadow the day before the derby. She was walking on a loose rein, sitting back casually in the saddle. Zoe caught up to her and they rode side-by-side for a while, of course not too close because of Gidget's tendency to get snarky.

Kendall was one of the nice ones—a kind, sweet girl. She was one of the few people on the circuit who seemed to have it all figured out—how to manage a successful career while having a semblance of a normal life at the same time. But you couldn't hate her for it—she was so damn nice. Even the fact that she was friendly to Zoe, and always had been, said a lot about her.

Kendall had never spent her time going out and partying, not even during her single days. Somehow she had always known not to get involved in that scene. She could have been terribly judgmental about the life Zoe had led but she wasn't.

They talked about their horses. Veracity was fifteen now. Kendall had won nearly every derby there was to win with him, including the Derby Finals the last two years. He was a bit of a big, plain horse, nothing flashy, but he jumped the crap out of the jumps. He probably could walk right into a CSI-3 and jump around clean—he had that much scope. These days Kendall saved him for only the biggest derbies.

They talked about their plans for the rest of the summer. Kendall wouldn't jump Veracity again after Genesee till Kentucky Summer. She'd show him in the derby classes there and then do the Derby Finals. "He knows his job," Kendall said. "All we try to do is keep him fit and happy."

Zoe told Kendall about how she really liked Gidget and thought she could be one of the good ones, maybe even one of the great ones. "I mean not as good as Veracity," she said. "But you know, she's pretty cool."

They turned back toward the stabling. The day was hot but it was the late afternoon and the air had cooled off just enough. Zoe spotted John outside the barn. Her heart lurched a little when she saw him.

Right then her life felt good. Almost too good to be true. She had a competitive horse, she was back doing big classes, she had a friend in Linda and even in Kirsten too, and a nice guy to spend time with and work with.

She said good-bye to Kendall and then closed her eyes for a few moments as she walked the rest of the way to the barn. She opened them again, glad that it was all still there—that it wasn't a dream. For the first time in a while, she felt truly hopeful. Hopeful that her life was changing. That good things were coming.

After untacking Gidget, she fed her her daily banana and stayed with her in her stall for a few minutes. The mare tolerated her now, maybe even liked her. "Aren't you going to give me one of your evil looks?" Zoe said to her.

Gidget finished her banana, making adorable smacking sounds with her lips from the banana mush.

"You got nothing for me today, huh?" Zoe said.

The next day only made Zoe's hopeful feelings grow. Gidget loved the meadow. She ate up the lines, her stride feeling expansive and powerful. Zoe was able to really ride forward, getting a true hunt course gallop. All the distances came up perfectly. It was one of those days where it felt like nothing could go wrong. Where every clover had four leafs. Where there wasn't a cloud in the sky.

Veracity went well too. He basically always went well. Zoe and Kendall had scores in the 90s in the first round, plus their high option points added in.

The handy had a trot jump. In a way, Zoe was glad. Gidget was going well over them at home and needed to prove that she could do it at a show. At home, Zoe had been alternating working her with and without the draw reins over the trot jumps. She thought she had figured out the exact measurement of leg and hand that she needed to keep Gidget together but that measurement worked at home and at Linda's. The different jumps and new surroundings would require a new calculation, and one that Zoe would have to determine in real time.

The handy started out with a few roll back turns and then a long approach to an in-and-out. Gidget jumped the in-and-out amazingly—Zoe could feel it over the jumps. She could also sense the crowd watching and admiring Gidget's scope and style.

She brought her back to the trot a little bit earlier than she might have with another horse but she wanted enough time to establish her pace and frame. She lowered her post just a

little, keeping her body quiet. Gidget was nicely on the bit for
a hunter—nose tucked in just enough, and neck rounded. Zoe
had a steady but light feel on her mouth.

She was a few feet out now. Zoe saw the distance, choosing a waiting distance so as not to have to push Gidget and
risk her breaking into the canter. She kept her leg on at take-
off and this time Gidget didn't stick off the ground. Zoe only
hoped she kept her form over the jump.

She rode the last few fences and finished to lots of ap-
plause. She could pick John's whoop out of the host of other
cheers.

Her scores came in a little lower overall than Zoe had expected and she couldn't help but feel a surge of disappointment. She asked John as she came out of the ring if Gidget
had lost her form over the trot jump or if anything else had
looked different than it felt to Zoe. He said he thought she
jumped super.

She did get all the handy points, which still put the pressure squarely on Kendall as the last to go in the class. As
Kendall entered the ring, Zoe thought how she really wanted
to win. She started to imagine herself accepting the blue
ribbon and Kendall congratulating her.

Yet as she and John watched Kendall, Zoe could honestly
say she wasn't rooting for Kendall to mess up. She liked her
too much for that.

Gidget had gone amazingly—Zoe told herself that was all
that she could ask for. And she'd rocked the trot jump.

The four judges were some of the best judges on the circuit—they all knew Zoe's story and she had to be proud that

they'd seen how well she had ridden and what a nice horse she was riding.

Whether she was first or second, the circuit would be buzzing and for the first time in a long while the buzz surrounding her would be positive.

When the scores came in, Kendall had beaten her, but only by a few points. Zoe shared a fleeting look of disappointment with John but then there was nothing but pride in what they'd accomplished with an unknown horse in a short amount of time.

"You rode super," he told her.

"It was all her today," Zoe said, meaning Gidget.

After the award ceremony, Zoe hugged Kendall.

"What a nice horse you've got yourself, girl," Kendall said.

They were interviewed by a writer for the *Chronicle* and when the issue came out, Linda showed it to Zoe the second she got to Morada Bay.

Zoe had been written up in the *Chronicle* plenty of times before and she'd already seen the coverage of the show online but somehow it was always a little different seeing it in print. She sat down on a tack trunk and read the article word for word. Kendall might have won the class and taken home the biggest check, but Zoe got most of the coverage in the article.

She had decided to be honest about everything in the interview, and not try to hide how she'd struggled mightily the past year. Everyone on the horse show circuit knew it already and most importantly, John knew it too.

The reporter had been amenable to whitewashing what

Zoe had done or leaving it out of the article completely. In fact, when Zoe had told her it was okay to put in that she'd been involved with the saddle stealing, the young woman had said, "Really? Are you sure you want that in there?"

"It's fine," Zoe had said. "It's the truth."

Veracity Edges Out Girl Next Door to Win Genesee Hunter Derby

The win could have gone either way at the Genesee Country Valley $35,000 International Hunter Derby on June 28. Two horses in very different stages of their careers matched scores throughout both rounds with the venerable derby horse, Veracity, ridden by Kendall Adams barely besting newcomer, Girl Next Door, with Zoe Tramell in the irons.

Blake Wickwire built a beautiful course that suited the Great Meadow where what has become a rider-favorite international derby takes place. Both Adams and Tramell took all the high options, feeling complete trust in their horses' ability.

"Veracity has so much scope I pretty much always take the high options," said Adams of Mt. Airy, N.C. "I can't even think of a time I haven't taken the high options in the past few years with him. He's such an old pro."

This year, Adams is choosing a limited schedule for Veracity, 15, saving him for the biggest classes. She's aiming for a third win at the Derby Finals in August.

If Veracity is an old pro, Girl Next Door is the ingénue. "Gidget" as she's called around the barn, belongs to John Bradstreet, a trainer out of Bedford, N.Y. Tramell started riding Gidget for Bradstreet when she moved to Bedford this spring to work at The Narrow Lane, a therapeutic riding program as community service for her involvement in a saddle stealing ring during the Winter Equestrian Festival. "I made some big mistakes during the winter and at first I wasn't exactly excited about working at Narrow Lane but it's been the most amazing experience and it's made me such a better person," Tramell explained.

She met Bradstreet, whose younger sister rides at Narrow Lane, and the two began talking about a promising young mare he had. Bradstreet invited Tramell to take Gidget for a spin and she knew immediately the mare had promise. "John does a super job picking horses. He really knows what he's looking for and what makes a top horse," she said. "Maybe it took me saying Gidget was that good to convince him she could do this well at this level but he should get all the credit because he's the one who picked her out and brought her along."

Arnie Aneletto, one of the judges for the Genesee Derby, agreed that Gidget has what it takes to compete with the likes of Veracity. "Both horses went super. Veracity never gives a bad jump that I've ever seen, and the mare matched him jump for jump," he said. "That mare has a lot of promise. She could be a regular winner in these classes. She has the stride and the scope and Tramell rides her great. She's always been a very talented rider."

For his part, Bradstreet was overwhelmingly happy with second place. He said, "To finish second in this class is a big deal for this horse and to come that close to beating Veracity I think says a lot about what kind of rider Zoe is. She's put the finishing touches on the mare and we wouldn't be standing here if it wasn't for her."

Bradstreet showed Gidget a few times the previous year, but he says he'd rather have Tramell in the saddle. "No contest," he laughed. "I'm not half the rider she is. She's got an amazing feel and the horses just love her. She brings out the best in every horse she sits on."

When the season began, Bradstreet hadn't planned on Gidget showing at Derby Finals. But the mare qualified with a second place finish in the International Derby held at Old Salem in May. Now he and Tramell have the finals in their sights. "There won't be any expectations," Bradstreet said.

Hopefully we'll get a rematch between these two talented horses.

Zoe scanned back through the article to reread the quotations about her, especially the one where Arnie said she rode Gidget great and that she was talented. It felt like he was speaking to her through the magazine, encouraging her.

Like so many of the judges on the circuit, he had known her forever, and he'd always liked her. He'd judged several big classes she'd won as a junior, including Junior Hunter Finals and one year at Washington when she was named Best Child Rider.

Too often she felt like the horse show world was against her, like people even wanted her to fail. Maybe that was just her projecting her own fears on them, her own worries about her self-worth—something her counselor had brought up to her—but it was reassuring to know that at least Arnie was rooting for.

And then there was what John had said about her. She glanced back over his words and let herself bask in them.

"Well?" Linda said.

Zoe had nearly forgotten Linda was still standing there, waiting for her to finish reading.

Linda readjusted her sunglasses on her head. "Pretty good, huh?"

"Really nice," Zoe said. "I'm almost teary. What Arnie said? And John?"

"Did you want them to write about the saddle stuff?" Linda asked.

"Yeah, I told the reporter it was fine. I guess I've decided I'd rather own up to things than try to hide them, you know?"

Linda gritted her teeth. "Yeah, I wish I could take a lesson from you . . ."

"You still haven't told him?"

"I'm going to. In Lake Placid. I'm telling him like first thing." Linda motioned to the magazine. "That was the right thing to do."

"Thank you," Zoe said. "That means a lot to me coming from you."

"Coming from the woman who won't tell her boyfriend she's pregnant with his child?" Linda joked.

"Well, there is that . . .."

Chapter 19

THERE WERE HORSE SHOWS that were just that—horse shows. No special setting, no cute town, no character to the show grounds. They were the food you ate because you were hungry, not because it tasted good.

And then there were the shows everyone looked forward to each year. Lake Placid was one of those shows.

You had the sheer beauty of the mountains surrounding you and there was also the charming town full of stores selling carved moose and bear decorations, maple syrup and maple syrup candy, chocolates in the shape of moose and bears, and red flannel pajamas.

Horse show people didn't tend to vacation much, so shows like Lake Placid took on double duty. They were busman's holidays.

Even if you didn't ever walk around Mirror Lake, hike the trails on Whiteface Mountain, or take the elevator to the top of the Olympic ski jump, you still felt as if you benefitted subliminally from those activities. You knew you could have done those things, and maybe would next year.

Restaurants abounded, as did bars. It wasn't just the horse show people that were in the bars either; hockey teams came to train at the Olympic Center. Bars and other athletes letting loose were often a dangerous combination, for junior riders especially. *Lake Plastered*, people had taken to calling the show years ago. As Zoe drove behind John pulling the trailer, she thought back to a crazy night with a hotshot young hockey player from Toronto.

John had never been to Lake Placid and Zoe felt like she was showing him a national monument. She hoped he'd think it was as great as she did, that he'd see it the same way she did. After they'd gotten the horses unloaded and settled in, she flooded him with information, rattling off restaurant names and things to do as if she was a tour guide.

She'd only done half of the things she mentioned herself but the way she said them made it seem like all anyone ever did in Lake Placid was go on excursions. She pointed out the ski jumps, which were visible from the show grounds on a clear day.

John seemed suitably impressed but at the same time more concerned with the show schedule, eager to map out what Gidget, Cruz, and Dibs would do each day. They had the use of Linda's golf cart when she didn't need it and Zoe had also picked up an old mountain bike with a free sign on it she'd seen on the side of the road back home so she wouldn't have to hoof it between the barn and the rings. Her bike wasn't glamorous but it beat walking.

Once the horses had all been ridden and the following day's schedule mapped out on the whiteboard, John and Zoe drove over to the hotel in their separate cars. John had made the hotel arrangements. Linda had told John the Pearces would pay half of Zoe's room since she was also working for them. Linda and Dakota were sharing a condo with a friend of Dakota's. Linda had said if they hadn't arranged the condo so far ahead of time they would have definitely planned for an extra room for Zoe. Most years she had stayed in condos with families that rode with Jamie.

Zoe worried all John could afford would be a super low budget motor lodge by the side of the road with crusty carpets and hair in the tub, but it was a Hampton Inn. Nothing amazing, but hopefully it would be sanitary.

She pulled her two bags out of the backseat and they headed into the lobby. There was a line at the counter, including a mom with a pony rider in breeches. Zoe stood slightly off to the side so no one might mistake her and John for a couple.

A few minutes passed as the people in front of them checked in. Zoe noticed packs of men and women in casual business attire flowing through the lobby. Zoe recalled that there was a big conference center in Lake Placid. One year there had been tons of people from a conference on STDs. That had provided fodder for lots of jokes at the horse show.

John was now talking to the person behind the desk.

"We have you down for one room," Zoe heard the young man, probably recently graduated from college with a degree in hotel management, say.

"No, two rooms. Bradstreet. Two rooms."

Zoe pivoted back to look at the front desk.

"Let me check again for you, Mr. Bradstreet," the man

said, leaning close to the computer. His nametag pinned to his cheap suit jacket said Travis. "I'm sorry but I only have the one room."

"Okay, well, that doesn't matter," John told Travis. "Can you just get us another room so we have two rooms?"

Zoe could hear John's voice turning tense. He was probably feeling badly. He wasn't paying her to ride—the least he could do was not screw up the room arrangements.

"I'm sorry, sir, we're all booked. We have a dental association here for the next several days and then a teacher's group coming in for continuing education."

"You're all booked, totally full, not one other room available?" John said, his voice now somewhere between suspicious and angry.

"Not one room. You can call around to other hotels in the area . . ."

Zoe stepped forward. "It's fine, really," she said to John. "Does the room have two beds?" she asked Travis.

"Yes, two beds," Travis replied. He looked happy Zoe had intervened but also like he was trying to figure out the relationship between them.

Zoe said, "It has two beds. What's the big deal? Think of all the money you'll save. We can go out to a nice dinner one night instead."

Zoe didn't even care about a nice dinner. She just wanted to make John less stressed.

"I can call around to other hotels," John told her.

"Why bother? I'm fine with it so unless you're not . . ."

It was a game of chicken now. He would have to be the

one to say that it made him feel uncomfortable to sleep in the same room with her.

"It's fine with me, too," he said.

Travis was following their conversation with a hopeful expression. "So we're all good?" he chanced to say.

Both Zoe and John said at the same time, "Yes."

They rode the elevator with two women attending the dental conference. One held a three-ring binder with a photo on the front of smiling teeth without a face, an image that was meant to be whimsical yet looked slightly creepy. Zoe thought how strange the world was. You could go into the dental profession and spend your whole life looking into people's mouths, or you could go into riding and spend your life on the back of a horse. Each world had its own in-crowd, its own lingo, its own culture.

The women stepped off at the second floor. At the fourth floor, Zoe pulled her rolling bag out with her other, smaller bag slung over her shoulder. "We can stay up late and do each other's nails, watch chick-flicks, it'll be a regular slumber party," she joked.

"Are you really sure you're okay with this?" John said as they arrived at the room and he was about to slide the credit card key through the slot.

"Should I not be? Are you going to have a hard time keeping your hands off me?" She meant to diffuse what was an awkward situation, but she realized as she said it, that it just made her feel more uncomfortable because she had come on to him that one night and he'd plainly turned her down.

"Yeah, it's going to be brutal," he said. "I'm gonna be

walking around the room the whole time trying to hide my boner."

She laughed, out of even more discomfort and because it was a slightly raunchy kind of humor she hadn't expected from him. Maybe there was a whole other side to him she'd be coming to know.

She worried it might just make her like him even more.

"Yeah, right," she said, laughing it off.

He slid the key through and the light blinked green. The door opened on a not terribly large room with, as promised, the two beds. Why did the beds seem so close to each other?

She deposited her shoulder bag on a chair and wheeled her bigger bag against the wall. She and Jed had stayed together in hotel rooms plenty of times before but he was gay and that made it different. They *had* painted each other's nails and watched chick-flicks. The only other men she'd been in hotel rooms with were the ones she slept with.

This was going to be different, but she would do her damnedest to act like it was the no big deal she claimed it was. Maybe it wouldn't have been a big deal if she hadn't come on to him that night, if there wasn't a part of her that still wondered whether there could be something between them.

"I'm starving," John said. "How about dinner? Or do you have people you want to catch up with?"

A few of the people she'd seen had casually told her, "Let's grab dinner," but so far the texts weren't flying in.

"I'm up for dinner. I'll just take a quick shower."

"Cool. I'll meet you in the lobby. I'm going to go check out the gym."

Maybe he actually was going to work out while they were there, or he was just trying to make things more comfortable by getting out of the room while Zoe showered. She put on real clothes (nothing too nice—this wasn't a date, after all) and met him back in the lobby. They took his truck and settled on a casual restaurant. Afterward Zoe took John to the popcorn place and they looked at all the crazy flavors and shared a bag of kettle corn.

As they walked out of the store, John said, "I just don't get who buys beer-flavored popcorn."

"Or dill pickle," Zoe added, offering John the bag.

"I like beer but I don't want beer popcorn."

"I know," Zoe said. "I like pickles but I don't want pickle popcorn."

They stopped in at the show to check on the horses. Zoe loved the quiet of the tent at night—the horses munching hay or resting with their heads low. Gidget had her butt to the door and didn't make any movements to turn and face them, or even acknowledge their existence when they said hello to her.

"I like the horses that want to curl up in your lap," John said. "I know she's talented and I'm the one who bought her but I wish she'd be a little less prickly."

"Don't listen to him, girl," Zoe said to the mare. "You just keep doing your thing because it's totally working for you."

Zoe opened the stall door and confidently moved to stand closer to Gidget's neck. Gidget trusted her now—she seemed to understand Zoe was on her side and would never punish her for being ornery.

Gidget pinned her ears back and gave Zoe a sidelong glare.

"There's my girl," Zoe said. "Just wanted to make sure you were still alive in there."

She held out a few mints she'd pocketed from the hostess stand at the restaurant. Gidget gobbled them greedily, but wouldn't offer any extra thanks—not a nudge with her nose, or a single lick of her tongue. They picked out the stalls, checked water bucket levels, and tossed each horse an extra flake of hay.

"I'll see you tomorrow," Zoe said to her. "Get your beauty sleep."

Back at the hotel, she used the bathroom first. She took her medicine and made sure to stash the bottle deep in her toiletry kit so he wouldn't see it. She wished she'd brought real pajamas instead of just a T-shirt and old leggings. She hadn't thought she'd be sharing a room with him.

She and John passed on his way into the bathroom and her way to get into bed. The space between the foot of the beds and the dresser was narrow and Zoe had to turn sideways, just barely brushing up against him. They exchanged a quick, charged glance.

"Sorry," John said. "Tight quarters."

"You're fine," Zoe said, feeling heat rise up her cheeks.

She was looking at her phone, scrolling through her Instagram feed, when John came out of the bathroom.

She wished he didn't look so good in his boxers and T-shirt. Right before he climbed into bed he pulled off his shirt. She glimpsed his chest, and a sprinkling of dark hair. She had to make herself stare at her phone.

How hard would it be to crawl into his bed? How could he possibly turn her down if she slipped off her own shirt and pressed herself against him?

No, she wouldn't. No way.

"Good-night," he said, turning off the one remaining light.

"Good-night. Hope your perpetual boner doesn't keep you awake all night!"

It felt like a risky thing to say, like it might fall flat and reveal her as being totally inappropriate. But she went for it. Was it an invitation? Maybe.

But he didn't seem tempted.

"I think I'll be okay," he replied.

She put down her phone, the ringer off, and turned on her side so she was facing the opposite direction of his bed. She stared at the dark room for a while, her eyes wide open, not sleepy in the slightest. She could hear him breathing and then his sheets rustle as he repositioned himself.

She thought of how he was shirtless and closed her eyes tight and told herself just to stop and find a way to go to sleep. Was he awake? Or was he already asleep? Was he thinking about her?

Minutes passed. She was still awake, but she was trying not move around so it'd seem like she was asleep. She couldn't figure out whether he was asleep or not. He probably was. Why did guys always have a way of sleeping much more soundly than women? They fell asleep the moment their head hit the pillow at night.

Women were the ones who stayed up reading or watching

TV. But maybe he actually was still awake. She considered asking him, *Are you awake? Can you sleep? Maybe this sharing a room wasn't such a good idea after all. I'm gonna ride like shit tomorrow. How's your boner?*

Random thoughts flew through her head. She decided saying nothing would be better than anything she might come up with.

She rolled over a few times, now rustling her own sheets on purpose, wondering if that would signal to him that she wasn't asleep and maybe he'd say something.

Nothing.

Sometime later in the night, mercifully, she fell asleep and slept clear through to being woken by the alarm on his phone.

He got right out of bed and traipsed to the bathroom. She could see his shirtless form in the dim light of the room. She listened to the water running and felt tired from falling asleep so late.

"You waking up?" he asked softly when he came out of the bathroom.

She liked the tender sound of his voice. "Yup, I'm up."

"I'll meet you in the lobby," he said. "I'm going to see what they have for coffee."

"Get me whatever they have," she said.

"Of course," he said. "I know how you love your coffee."

Chapter 20

"YOU WERE RIGHT about packing warm clothes," John said, putting an arm into the sleeve of a North Face puffy jacket.

Mornings in Lake Placid were chilly and for the first few hours of the day it hardly looked like July as riders rode by bundled up in down jackets and vests with scarves wrapped around their necks.

John had just thrown grain and was pulling out a wheelbarrow to start stalls. Zoe came to block his path. "I made a little deal with Linda," she said.

"And what's that?"

"She really can't ride with her back. I said you'd help me get all of Dakota's horses ridden and prepared if she got one of the guys to clean your stalls."

"I don't mind cleaning my stalls. I actually kind of like it," John said, his hands still on the wheelbarrow.

"You can clean them again this afternoon if you want," Zoe said. "She really needs our help. This isn't just for you. We're doing this for her."

It was mostly true. Linda hadn't told anyone else she was pregnant yet and Zoe felt protective of her. People rode through their pregnancy—hell, some grand prix riders jumped in 5-star classes through their fifth or sixth month—but Linda had a bad back *and* she was pregnant.

There was no way she should be riding.

"Fine," John said. "If it helps Linda, okay."

The morning passed quickly with all the riding that needed to be done. Zoe and John rode out together, flatted in the same ring usually, and then rode back together. As always, Zoe passed endless people who said *hello* and *how's it going* to her. A few people even remembered John's name and asked if the mare would be showing this week.

Zoe made sure to introduce John any chance she got and she also tried her best to subtly work into any short conversation that he had brought some sale horses. By the time all of Dakota's horses and all of John's were ridden, she had managed to give out John's number to one trainer who said he would text later about watching Cruz, and told another trainer that she should try Dibs.

"I noticed you didn't mention Gidget's for sale," John said.

"I think her value's only going to go up this summer," Zoe said with a slight smile. "Better to wait."

"I agree," John said.

Dakota had a lesson on Plato and flatted Midway and Sonny. The rest of the time, she hung out around the horse show. There were a lot of fun classes to watch and a lot of fellow juniors to hang out with. Every time Zoe saw Dakota she seemed to be surrounded by a group of juniors, talking closely, looking at each other's phones, piled on a golf cart that some older junior who had a license was driving.

A few times she saw her with Ian, Hugo's working student, who had ridden Plato at Old Salem. Later, she asked her, "You staying true to our pact?"

"Totally. You?"

"I've been like a nun."

Dakota giggled.

"Lake Placid can be trouble," Zoe said, turning more serious.

"I know. A bunch of people were talking about going out tonight . . ."

"You have a fake ID?"

Dakota nodded, like she wasn't sure she should be admitting this to Zoe.

"Be careful, okay? You can call me anytime," Zoe said. "I'm not going to say, don't go out, because I'm not a total hypocrite, but be careful."

"I will. I'm just going to stay with my friends."

"But they suddenly might not stay with you . . ." Zoe knew all too well how people paired up and peeled off, and Dakota could be left alone, easy prey for just the kind of guy she was trying to avoid.

"I know."

"If you need a ride home. If you need anything. Just text me or call me. I'm going to be sitting in my hotel room watching a movie. No bars for me."

John rode Cruz in a 1.20 meter class. Zoe helped him school and she could tell he was a little nervous at the in-gate, just a little impressed by the jumper ring. The jumps weren't big and the course wasn't tricky, but it was a large ring with impressive grandstands with flags flapping in the ever-present Adirondack breeze, and sponsorship banners along the fence line.

Despite what might have been a few nerves, John marched Cruz right around, riding it like an eq course. Cruz was a little rough through his change in a corner of the ring, tossing his head, and John trained him, making him listen and flex before the next jump.

The trainer Zoe had told about Cruz had come to watch him go. Brett Kirschner was from Maryland and had been around the circuit for what seemed like forever. He always had a full barn and lots of clients but none ever quite made it to the top. He was also flamingly gay.

"Nice, huh?" Zoe said to Brett. "Green, needs a little more polish and mileage, but nice."

Zoe wasn't used to brokering deals. She had certainly listened to Jamie and others endlessly pitching horses, extolling their virtues. She knew the lingo to throw around: *endless scope, big step, no spook, little prep, no stop, great mind, good attitude, great look, super sound.*

Now it was her turn to use those same words but she wasn't sure she would be as good at pulling it off. She decided to try to differentiate John from some of the other horse dealers out there.

"John's the real deal. No devices or gimmicks. He's been putting solid basics and flatwork into this horse. This isn't a 'fluff and buff' and turn around and sell it. John brings along his horses slowly and so you know what you're seeing is real, and not just some band-aid effect."

As she talked, Zoe's confidence grew. She found it all exciting—the arranging the time and place, the showcasing the horse, the carefully planned words.

She guessed it wouldn't feel as good if she were someone like Donnie, trying to pass off a half-sound horse that had been lunged or, even drugged, into submission. How could people like Donnie do what they did—sell horses they knew weren't as advertised?

They had to sell *some* good ones, or else they'd never make another sale again. It was just every so often they pulled one over on a clueless buyer. They picked and chose whom to fleece. Established trainers they'd see every day and who would even judge them, they didn't mess with.

It was the smaller no-name trainers who thought they were oh-so-cool taking a client who actually had money to someone like Donnie to buy a horse. Zoe used to feel nothing but distaste for those rubes, but now she felt her heart go out to them. Those trainers and clients didn't know any better.

John had jumped the last few fences and was on the way out of the ring. He didn't have any rails down but because he was going for the equitation school he had multiple time faults.

"When can I try him?" Brett said to Zoe.

It was all she could do not to give a little squeal. "What works for you?"

* * *

Brett tried Cruz a few hours later. The sun had warmed up the showgrounds and all around people were peeling off layers and tucking them in ring bags and golf carts. The rider he had for Cruz was pretty damn good but didn't have much money—well, not in horse show terms, anyway. In real life terms, her family was comfortably well-off.

But because she didn't have half a million dollars floating around to put toward a proven eq horse, she'd have to make due with a greenie. She had three more years left in the eq, including this one, so they had decided it made the most sense to invest all their money in a horse that could end up being the real deal, instead of spreading out the 150K they had to spend on three years of leasing a mediocre eq horse and then have nothing to show for it money-wise at the end.

This route meant a possible payoff. If they did a good job bringing Cruz the rest of the way and he stayed sound—and there was no reason he shouldn't—and if she got ribbons on him at the finals, they could be looking at 200K to 300K in their pocket.

"We've looked at a lot of horses," Brett admitted. "The shit people try to sell you, I swear."

"John's really selective in what he buys," Zoe said, nodding effusively. "And he puts a lot of work into his horses. Cruz is really ready to go to the next level."

Zoe noticed a few other trainers noticing her, noticing that she had a nice horse that was being tried.

The girl rode Cruz nicely. She kept patting him, which Zoe took to mean she liked him. Brett fielded three phone calls while she was trying him—often saying one thing into the phone and then calling out to the girl, "Jump the oxer," and then going back to whoever was on the phone. He kept calling the people he was talking to dear and sweetie.

Once when he was still on a call, he said to Zoe, "I want to talk to the parents, probably have him vetted. You have X-rays?"

"Yup," Zoe said.

"You showing him to anybody else today, dear?" Brett asked, with the phone still pressed to his ear. Into the receiver he said, "Yes, I know it's a dog. I told her it was a dog when she showed up at my barn with it."

Brett held the phone out and made an exaggerated face for Zoe and John's benefit.

Zoe said, "We'll give you first right of refusal."

"Yup, sweetie, bye," Brett said into the phone. He clicked off and then told Zoe and John, "I like the horse. I'll be back to you ASAP."

The girl rode Cruz up to them and hopped off. She patted his neck again.

"You like him, right, darling?" Brett said to her.

"A lot," she replied.

"I know. He's a good one for you. We'll see if we can get it done, sweetie."

The girl handed the reins to Zoe.

Brett said, "A hundred and thirty, right?"

"One-fifty," Zoe said. She knew she had said one-fifty.

"Don't we have some leeway?" Brett said.

"Not really," Zoe said.

"Do we have to take care of you on this, dear?" Brett said.

"No," Zoe said. "One-fifty is with everyone taken care of."

"Okay." He leaned a little closer to her. "So, girl, what about you and Donnie? Are you like totally done with that fuckwit?"

"Totally done with him."

"Do you know he sold a client of mine a horse that was nerved? Before she came to me, of course. Oh my God, nerved! Can you believe that, dear? They had no idea."

"Sadly, I can believe it," Zoe said.

"Good for you for getting out of that situation," Brett said. "You be good to yourself now, sweetie."

"I will, I mean, I am," Zoe said.

Brett's phone buzzed again and he answered, waving to them and mouthing good-bye. John hopped back on Cruz and told Zoe he'd see her later.

"I'll come back to the barn," she said.

"You don't have to. I can take care of him."

"I know," she said. "But I don't mind."

"Okay," he said, as he headed out of the schooling ring.

Zoe got on her bike and pedaled back to the barn, passing John and Cruz on the way. At the tent, she got out the wash bucket and squirted a dash of shampoo in it. John rode up on Cruz and Zoe undid the girth and slid off the saddle while John slid on Cruz's halter.

"That certainly seemed to go well, *sweetie*," John said as he hung the bridle on the cleaning hook with the few others waiting there.

Zoe chuckled. "I know, and other people were watching so you're getting a secondary benefit of it too. People talk about what horse so-and-so just bought and from-who and pretty soon they'll be calling you up asking what you have available."

Zoe grabbed the bucket and reached for the lead rope that John was holding. "I'll take him out and wash him down."

"I can do it," he said. "Why should you?"

They both held the lead rope, and they laughed because it was as if they were going to have a tug-of-war to see who would get the privilege of washing down Cruz.

"You didn't feel like I took over too much out there, I mean with Brett?" Zoe asked.

"No, you're the one who knows these people and you know what to say, what they want to hear. It makes sense that you do more of the talking."

"I just hope you don't feel like I don't think you could handle it or something?"

"It's fine, *dear*," John said. "We're a good team."

"I know, who would have thought?"

"What do you mean? You wouldn't have thought we'd be good partners?"

Zoe's hand was still on the lead rope. "We didn't get off on the best foot when we first met if you recall . . ."

"And you're like miss super-star and I'm just this guy with a few horses for sale."

"Don't put yourself down. You have a small sales operation. You have really nice horses. One that we're about to sell for a nice chunk of change."

Cruz had been waiting pretty patiently but he lifted a leg

and pawed the ground once, as if he was just trying to remind them he was here, waiting to be put away.

"Maybe I'm like the marketing department of our sales operation?" Zoe said.

John gave a playful tug on the lead rope. "Our?"

"Too soon?" she said, cocking her head flirtatiously.

"Maybe a little." He took his free hand and used it to literally pry her fingers off the lead rope. "I've got this one, *sweetie*."

"Fine, I'll clean some tack, *darling*."

Now that it was time to move, Cruz didn't want to anymore and John had to nudge his shoulder and cluck to get him going down the aisle to the wash rack.

Zoe got the tack bucket and headed out behind him. He was filling his bucket and she placed her bucket on the ground next to his.

"Following me?" he said, over the spray of the hose.

"I need water? To clean the tack?" She motioned to her bucket as his was almost filled, full of frothy bubbles.

Cruz reached out to sniff the buckets, as if they might be filled with something more interesting than water.

"You wanna get dinner tonight?" he said.

"Sounds great," she said.

"Maybe we could even watch a movie. I know it seems kind of wrong to be watching something without Molly but I heard about a really good one where a girl needs a wedding dress and she falls in love with the boyfriend of the wedding planner, who's also really a maid by the way, whose best friend is really in love with the guy the girl who needs the wedding dress is supposed to marry, but the girl who needs the wedding dress thinks he's . . ."

"Stop, please," she said, taking the hose out of his hand.

Chapter 21

THE REST OF THE afternoon she wondered if things were changing between them. It sure felt like it. It felt like something more than friendship was taking root.

But maybe it was just the glow coming off their success with Gidget and now with the possible sale of Cruz. Brett had called to arrange the vetting. It was possible that before long money would be transferred and Cruz would be leaving Lake Placid in a different van than the one he'd come in.

Zoe was busy that afternoon helping Linda with Dakota in the equitation so she didn't see much of John. She spotted him watching the schooling area for the grand prix field during the $20,000 1.40 meter open stake class. It was smart of him not to watch the class itself but to study the schooling area, to watch how the top riders prepared their horses. It was probably more of an education than watching the actual class.

While the Maclay was flatting, she got a text from Morgan, of all people.

Wanna hang out tonight?

She looked at her phone and back up to the class. Dakota had put in a good trip with Plato and she still needed Maclay points. She looked good on the flat. If anything she'd probably move up a spot or two. One of the girls who had also been good was short and a little stocky.

The equitation kind of sucked in that if you weren't built for it you had an uphill battle. Zoe had been built for it and Dakota was too. The stocky girl was a good rider but she nearly always slipped a spot or two in the flat, and even over fences her look detracted from her talent.

Zoe glanced at her phone again, rereading the text. What the hell was she supposed to do? She had said she'd have dinner with John, but they could have dinner any night, and if she had dinner with him she'd wish that something more would happen and then she might throw herself at him again. And he'd likely turn her down again.

It was better to keep it platonic, she told herself. They were good partners—business partners. They were working well together and if she could just keep that up, keep building her visibility in the show ring, it was only a matter of time before a position opened up riding at a big barn again.

Maybe she'd still be able to agent some of his horses once she was at a bigger barn. He could even send them to her to get sold once he'd put the work into them.

If they went out tonight she could see it now: things would get all weird, and he'd decide he wasn't going to the big shows anymore. Just like that, she'd have lost her one good ride and a chance at a good job again.

She decided to write back to Morgan. *Are you here?*

Coming tonight. Doing the GP Sunday.

It must be nice to be Morgan. Of course his horses were already at the show, being prepared by his trainer. He'd cruise on in and jump in the biggest class at the show.

Okay, she wrote back. It was one little word but it felt like a pretty big decision.

And maybe the wrong one.

The riders were called to the middle of the ring. Shortly thereafter, the results were announced.

Dakota finished second. It was a good ribbon, even though it was late in the qualifying season and most of the really top riders were already qualified. She was now qualified for the Regionals, and it also qualified her for the Kathy Scholl equitation class at the end of the show for riders who placed first or second in any of the big eq classes.

The mood was jovial as she and Linda zoomed back to the tent in the golf cart.

"That's a load off," Linda said. "We're all set except for the Talent Search, which, if it happens, great, if it doesn't, she's still young and it's not the total end of the world."

"What horse will you use at the Talent Search Finals? You won't use Dudley or Plato?"

"No, she'll probably ride Logan actually."

"That's a good call. He's super brave and rideable."

Zoe almost added that there was a time when those things certainly wouldn't have been said about Logan but she stopped herself since Linda didn't need to know the whole history of Logan before Dakota had bought him. "Hannah would think that Logan doing the Talent Search was super cool."

"How is Hannah?" Linda asked. "Talk to her lately?"

"We text but we don't talk all that much. I think she kind of needs to separate herself from the horse shows for a while and maybe talking to me makes it harder to do."

"I get that. When I stopped doing the horses for a while, I didn't want to talk to anyone that was still in it. Does she talk to Chris?"

"No. Well, not that I know of anyway."

"Did you see the team won at St. Gallen?"

They passed Callie in her golf cart, her two Shiba Inu dogs riding shotgun. Both Linda and Zoe waved.

"Yeah, I saw the photos. Chris and Mary Beth together, smiling like crazy. I hope Hannah unfollowed all horse-related social media."

"Do you think they're back together?" Linda asked.

"Probably. I mean they're in Europe together all summer, at the same shows, on the same team."

Linda made a face. "I hope Chris has better sense then to take back up with her."

"Me too, but you know guys."

They pulled up to the tent. Zoe had forgotten for a few moments that she had to tell John she couldn't have dinner with him. He was wrapping Cruz.

"How'd Dakota do?" he asked.

"Second. Now she's all qualified, except for the Talent Search. It'd be great if she could knock that one off her list to-morrow."

"Linda must be relieved," John said.

"Very."

"So where do you want to eat?" John stood up. He was suddenly close to her, and she didn't know how she was going to tell him. She could cancel with Morgan. But no, she had to stick to her plan. Platonic. Keep it platonic.

"Actually, I saw an old friend up at the ring—"

"Oh, no problem," John said immediately, turning distant and professional. "I totally get it."

"Raincheck?" Zoe said.

John moved past her to retrieve two more wraps and bent down next to Cruz's back legs. "Yeah, sure, whatever."

"I was looking forward to it," Zoe said.

"You don't have to feel badly." John positioned the cotton and started with the wrap. "It's no big deal."

He looked totally and completely focused on his wrapping job, as if he was a Pony Clubber and this was the first time he'd been authorized to wrap his horse himself.

Zoe tried to think of something else she could say. But what was there to say, really?

"Okay, thanks for understanding," she said.

* * *

Zoe came out of the bathroom, wet hair up in a towel, turban-style, and another towel tucked under her arms. She had forgotten her underwear when she'd brought her clothes with her into the bathroom. She leaned over to retrieve them from her bag, feeling the skimpy hotel towel ride up and reveal her upper thigh and even a bit more. She peeked around and caught John looking. He whipped his head back to his iPad and she scampered back into the bathroom, clutching her underwear in a tight ball.

She was in the bathroom for a while longer and when she came out, John picked his eyes up from the iPad again. She had on white capri jeans and a cute top.

"Would this old friend happen to be a male?" he asked.

"Yeah, but it's not like that." The moment the words were out of her mouth she was kicking herself. Someone might see her out with Morgan and it would get back to John. If there was nothing between her and John, why didn't she just tell him the truth?

To change the subject, she said, "What are you doing for dinner?"

"I think I'm just going to walk around Main Street. Grab something easy. I want to look in a few stores—find something to bring back for Molly."

And now he had to go and be all sweet, taking the time to shop for Molly.

"When are you meeting this old friend?"

"You can stop saying old friend," she said.

"Okay, when are you meeting your friend?" he asked.

"Soon," she said.

In reality, she hadn't heard anything from Morgan since the text. For all she knew, he'd stand her up.

"Where are you going?"

"I don't know yet. We're going to figure that out."

John grabbed his wallet and keys. "Okay, well, have fun. I won't wait up."

"Haha," she said.

After John had left, the room felt very quiet. An hour passed with no communication from Morgan. Zoe's stomach growled. She made sure her phone was working. Yup. No missed calls that somehow she didn't hear come in.

Reflecting back on his text, he'd said, *wanna hang out tonight*? He hadn't said anything about dinner. She'd just kind of assumed as much. He hadn't even said *when* he was arriving.

She went down to the hotel lobby and bought an energy bar and a sad looking apple at the tiny hotel store, brought them up to the room, and ate them while continuing to stare at her phone. She could text or call him. But she didn't want to seem needy.

She could text John and see if he'd eaten yet. But that would mean announcing that she'd been stood up. Sitting right where he'd left her when he got back would also mean announcing she'd been stood up so she decided to go wait in her car. But she couldn't sit in her car in the front of the parking lot because he might see her there too. So she drove around to the back and waited as the sun went down.

Morgan finally texted at 9:20. *I'm here. Ordering room service. Come over?*

He was at the Mirror Lake Inn Resort and Spa. The most expensive hotel in the area, of course.

She made herself wait a full ten minutes before replying that she'd head over.

In all her years in Lake Placid, Zoe had never been inside the Mirror Lake Inn. The interior could have doubled as a millionaire's hunting lodge—wood-paneled walls, stone fire-places, and mounted trophies. Morgan's suite had a similar decor. She imagined what it would be like to stay at the best hotels at every horse show and get there often by private plane. It seemed pretty appealing.

After opening the door to let her in, Morgan sat back down at the table by the window, returning to his half-eaten steak.

"I got you soup," he said. "I didn't know if you'd want anything. I'm sure you already ate but soup's always good. You can order something else if you want?"

She felt oddly touched that he'd ordered her soup, or any-thing at all. "What kind is it?"

He took the cover off so she could see. "Vegetable barley. It looks pretty good."

He handed her a spoon and poured her a glass of wine. Maybe it was pathetic that ordering her one bowl of soup felt like a tremendously caring gesture. But it made her feel hope-ful about their relationship. They could be like the reverse of the couple in *The Best of Me*. She'd be the girl from the wrong side of the tracks who ends up with the popular, rich guy.

The soup was still steaming hot and tasted delicious, maybe just because after a long day of riding all she'd had was an energy bar and an apple and she'd spent the last hour sitting in the dark in her car.

"How's the show?" he asked.

"Great. I was champion in the high performance hunters and John and I are about to sell a horse, and I've been helping Linda with Dakota."

"Who's John?" Morgan asked.

Zoe took a moment to remember she hadn't seen or talked to Morgan in weeks and that he really knew nothing about her life. "He's the guy who owns the horse I do in the high performance and the derbies."

Morgan wiped his mouth and placed the napkin back on the table. "Is he gay?"

"Are you jealous?" She cocked her head.

"Should I be?"

"He's not gay," she said. "And we're just work partners."

Morgan shrugged. "I have no claim on you. What you do when I'm not around is your business."

It felt like more of a statement on what *he* did when she wasn't around. He might as well have said, *I sleep with whoever I want and you should too.*

The soup had made her feel like Morgan might actually care about her, and now she felt certain he didn't care about her.

Zoe stood up and walked around the expansive room. She picked up the TV card that listed the channels. "Wanna watch a movie?"

"You mean porn?" He came up behind her, positioning his hands on either side of her waist and drawing her close, essentially grinding his crotch against her ass. He put his lips to her neck and she felt his teeth against her flesh.

Please let him just be rubbing his teeth against me, and not about to bite me, she thought.

She turned to face him. It wasn't altogether easy to wriggle out of his grasp. "I actually meant a real movie, like a romantic comedy."

"I thought maybe you wanted to watch porn together."

"You *wished* I wanted to watch porn together. I was talking about something fun, like where the girl's marrying the wrong guy or something."

"No thanks," he said coolly. "I've got things in mind to do with you." He looked at her suggestively. "Are you wearing one of those tiny thongs?"

Damn it, she was, and now she wished she wasn't. She wished she was wearing baggy grandma undies the size of a pillow case. She wished she was so unsexy and they'd be forced to do something other than just fuck.

But it was all he wanted to do and she realized that resisting or trying to stall the inevitable was pointless. She let him kiss her. His kisses were all consuming, taking nearly her entire mouth in his.

His sexuality was overwhelming, like he didn't have a dimmer switch; it was either full on or nothing.

Her last sexual partners had been Donnie and Étienne. Donnie, she figured out, had a problem getting it up and much of the time with him at first was spent getting him hard, or dealing with the fact that he was only half-hard. Then he started to compensate by spending most of his time pleasing her. It was his way of avoiding the fact that he couldn't perform, which for a man who prided himself on being first in the show ring, was clearly intolerable.

Then there was Étienne. She had expected the sex to be totally hot since he was foreign. That he'd be sensual and able to make her orgasm just by licking her breast or something crazy like that. But in fact sex with him was rote. Lots of missionary that went on forever since the drugs he was on must have made him unable to climax. Half the time they ended up stopping.

Zoe's last two partners had been basically a sampling of sexual dysfunctions.

At first Morgan's attack-mode sensibility seemed appealing but now she felt too much like prey. He grabbed at her clothes again. To avoid him ripping them she pulled off her own shirt. He buried his head in her breasts. She ran her hands through his hair, and he groaned.

She relaxed for a moment, let her guard down, because right then their foreplay seemed normal, regular-unleaded. But she shouldn't have relaxed because suddenly he whipped his head up, scaring her with the sudden movement alone. Then he twisted her arm behind her back. She turned so he was behind her again, trying to get him to loosen his grip.

Instead he pushed her toward the wall and then slammed her against it. What was with him and walls? This time, it was her shoulder that took the brunt of the hit. He had let go of her other arm and she rubbed her throbbing shoulder.

"What the hell?" she said.

"Did I hurt you?"

She studied him, trying to assess whether he was serious. "Yes, it fucking hurt. When you slam someone into a wall, it usually hurts."

"I'm so sorry," he said, genuinely.

He hung his head in his hands for a few moments and it looked like he was crying. His shoulders were shaking. She couldn't believe he might actually be crying.

He looked at her, his eyes full of tears. "I am so sorry. I don't know why I did that."

She felt numb, unable to figure out what to do next since

things were happening so strangely and out of sequence that her brain felt scrambled and she couldn't find the appropriate emotion to have. What emotion should she feel when one moment he was slamming her against a wall, and the next he was crying and apologizing?

It was sexual whiplash.

He led her back to the bed, gently this time. He laid her down and slowly, carefully kissed every inch of her. He kept mumbling, "I'm sorry. I'm so sorry. I don't know what's fucking wrong with me. I'm fucking shit."

She shouldn't have felt badly for him but she did. She found herself mumbling back, "it's okay," when it really wasn't okay. The guy needed help.

And people thought *she* was messed up?

No one at the horse show would ever believe the shit Morgan had pulled with her. At the horse show he was the guy everyone liked. Some of the wealthiest people at the shows had professions that the rest of the show world barely understood. "Something to do with money management," was often an explanation bandied about for where so-and-so's money came from.

Morgan's wealth was easy to comprehend. His money came from his family owning a Major League baseball team. Not only was it concrete and quantitative, it was also pretty damn cool.

Anytime someone from the horse shows was in the real world and the Mets came up, they could say, "I actually know the owner's son. He rides." And people would be all impressed.

Then there was the fact that Morgan was a very good rider and had a gregarious personality. It was only alone with her that he was mercurial.

Everyone thought he was just a regular guy. Anyone who hadn't gone to bed with him, that is.

Or maybe he saved his dysfunction for Zoe.

For a while he'd dated the daughter of a wealthy real estate scion. It was hard for Zoe to believe he'd pulled this kind of shit with Blythe.

He was kissing along her hip bone now, moving lower.

She thought to herself, *what the hell is this*? Should she stop him?

She tried to relax and at least get something good out of this ordeal. She soon learned he was actually really adept at giving oral sex, which she felt was all wrong for someone as self-centered as he was. He was full of incongruities.

He knew how to bring her right up to the point of orgasm and then back off just ever so slightly. Not enough as to leave her stranded but just enough to make her cry out for him to keep going.

After she had finally come, he kneeled over her and went to work on himself, getting himself off. She wondered if she should ask him whether he wanted her to help but then figured he could take care of his own damn self. Plus, he seemed pretty into it.

He came onto her stomach and then lay down next her and sighed like the sequence of events that they'd been through was typical and not completely messed up.

He just slammed me against a wall, cried and apologized,

went down on me, and then left a puddle on my stomach.
Zoe's head was spinning. Just when she thought her life was getting slightly more stable and mundane, she had to go and get involved with Morgan Cleary.

Chapter 22

ZOE SLIPPED INTO the hotel room past midnight, trying to be quiet so as not wake John. When she got in bed she listened to his breathing to try to tell whether he was awake. She was pretty sure he was.

She woke the next morning to a text coming in and when she rolled over to get her phone her shoulder screamed with pain. She sat up and tested out moving her arm, grimacing as she tried to establish whether she'd be able to ride. It killed but somehow she'd make it happen.

The text was from John saying he'd gotten up even earlier and was at the show. She checked his bed—empty. Clearly he hadn't wanted to see her.

A shopping bag sat on the table by the window. Zoe couldn't resist seeing what he'd bought for Molly. She peeked inside at a plush, adorable stuffed moose. Her heart cracked a little at how sweet and normal he was.

She downed three ibuprofen and took a hot shower. Pulling on her shirt was a process. She only hoped the meds would kick in.

At the show the aisles in the tent felt suddenly narrow and she was hyper aware of trying to leave room between her and John as they passed. They spoke only of facts and logistics, what horses needed what preparation, who was showing when.

Things had changed.

The ibuprofen took enough of the edge off the pain so Zoe could hack Gidget. Still, she rode a lot to the right because it was the left shoulder that hurt. Going to the right, she could rely on her outside rein.

The outside rein was always the most important rein—something people just learning to ride didn't always understand. It was the rein that balanced a horse, that kept them regulated.

She passed Morgan when she was walking back on Gidget from the hunter schooling ring and he was walking up to the jumper ring on one of his beautiful horses.

He nodded casually at her like nothing had happened between them the night before and Zoe would have wondered if she had made the whole thing up if it weren't for her arm.

Dismounting back at the barn, she forgot about her shoulder for a moment and jumped off normally, hitting her shoulder against the saddle coming down and sending a wave of pain shooting through her body. She felt dizzy and the world blurred. She closed her eyes and leaned her forehead into the saddle flap for a moment, waiting to come back to herself. Thankfully, Gidget stood still, happy to relax for a moment.

"Are you okay?" John said, startling her.

She pulled away from Gidget, taking the reins over her head. "Yeah, I'm fine," she said, trying to ignore the pain and steady herself.

"Did something happen while you were riding?"

"Um, no." She tried to figure out what she could say happened. How could she explain this? "I just, this morning, you know when you wake up and you don't really know where you are? I had one of those moments and on the way into the bathroom I slammed my shoulder on the side of the door."

John narrowed his eyes at her like there was no way he was buying that one. "You hit your shoulder on the side of the door?"

"Don't you ever wake up and not know where you are? Like you're not sure if you're at home, or in a hotel, or a camper?"

"No, not really. I can't say I've ever had that happen."

"Well, that's because you don't go on the road all the time. I sleep in a different place like almost every five or six days. Sometimes I have no idea where I am anymore."

Her lie was gathering steam. It actually made sense that she wouldn't know where she was some nights given her crazy nomadic horse show life. She felt nearly proud of herself for coming up with such a good cover and selling it so convincingly. Well, she thought it was convincing; maybe John didn't.

"I think if you ask anyone what it's like living this life, they'd get what I'm talking about. Like Linda . . . she'd understand." Zoe led Gidget into the aisle and to the grooming stall.

"What would I understand?" Linda said, coming out of the junk stall.

"How when you go from horse show to horse show and hotel room to hotel room sometimes you wake up and have no idea where you are." Zoe prayed Linda would corroborate her story.

"That's happened to me from time to time," she said. "It's really kind of freaky."

"See?" Zoe said to John.

"Do you ever hit your shoulder on the doorframe of the bathroom so hard that you're wincing and holding back tears when you get off a horse?" John said to Linda.

Linda gave John a confused look, like she was realizing what she'd stumbled into was more than just a casual survey of the hazards of the horse show life.

"Um, I guess, no, that's never happened to me. But I usually just stay in bed and wait till I remember where I am." She glanced at Zoe. "You hurt your shoulder?"

"Yeah, it's fine, though. I'm fine."

"It looks fine," John said, raising his eyebrows and nodding sarcastically. "I'm going to get coffee. I know Zoe wants one. Linda?"

"No, thanks," Linda said.

When he was out of the tent, Linda said, "What the hell? You didn't really bang it on the doorframe. Please tell me this wasn't Donnie Rysman."

"No, it wasn't. I promise you. I'm never having anything to do with that asshole again."

"Okay? So? Then what happened?"

Zoe looked at the white ceiling of the tent. If there was anyone she could talk to, it was Linda. But she didn't even know how to go into some of the stuff that happened last night.

"It was a different asshole," she said.

Zoe double checked the aisle to make sure Dakota hadn't arrived yet. Zoe knew she had totally broken their pact. But breaking the pact seemed like the least of her problems right then.

"I was with Morgan Cleary. He's kind of rough in bed."

"There's a little rough . . . and then there's injured-rough," Linda said in a concerned voice. "Honey, this kind of rough is not okay."

"I know, I know. He was sorry after. He said he was sorry like a million times. He cried—I mean actually shed legit tears—when he realized he'd hurt me."

"That still doesn't make it okay. Please, trust me, I've been with guys like this. I know he's Morgan Cleary but he sounds fucked up and you need to stay away from him. You deserve so much better."

"I know," Zoe said. "I just thought like maybe it would work out between us and I know it's so shallow but can you imagine never having to worry about money ever again?"

"No, I can't," Linda said ruefully. "But trust me, I know so many people in this business who are loaded and are so unhappy. I thought maybe you and John? I thought I was picking up some vibes between you two?"

Zoe shook her head. "That's a total no-go. He's not interested."

"Really?"

"Really."

"How do you know?"

"Because I practically threw myself at him and anyway I'm not ruining what we have professionally."

"Well, that's probably smart, actually. So just stay away from Morgan and guys like him."

"I will. I'm going to."

"Are you really okay to ride?" Linda asked.

Zoe scrunched up her nose. "Could we put Midway on the lunge instead? He's perfect no matter what."

"Sure, we can."

"You're a lifesaver."

Linda reached out and hugged Zoe.

"Gentle," Zoe said.

She tried to detect whether she could feel Linda's baby bump. She was nearly three months pregnant but not showing as far as Zoe could tell, although Linda was often secretly complaining to Zoe how tight her breeches were and joking about whether maternity breeches existed.

"Sorry," Linda said, loosening her embrace.

"You're going to be such a great mom," Zoe said as they let go.

"Thank you," Linda said.

"Speaking of which . . ." Zoe said. "Have you told him?"

Linda had been going out nearly every night with Eamon and he often popped over to their tent to say hi and hang out for a few moments.

Zoe felt suddenly selfish that she hadn't asked Linda about whether she'd told him.

"No," Linda said.

"I thought you were going to."

"I *was*. But then I began to think, what if he wants to marry me?"

"And that would be bad because . . .?"

"I want to have this baby. I want to be a mother. And I thought I wanted to be married but I'm not sure I know Eamon that well. We went out for dinner and I found out he's allergic to shellfish. I didn't even know he's allergic to anything. I mean if he eats like one bite of shrimp his throat will swell up and he'll die. Like right there on the spot. I'm about to have a baby with someone that I didn't know could be killed by a shrimp. I just don't want to be one of those horse show people who gets knocked up, marries the guy, and a year or two later, boom, they're divorced. I want to make sure he's the one."

Zoe had never seen Linda so worked up. She was always composed and in control. Suddenly Zoe noticed Linda's trademark sunglasses weren't on her head.

"Wait, where are your sunglasses?"

"I left them at the hotel. Can you believe that? That's how freaked out I am right now. I mean how many times do you see me without my sunglasses?"

"Like never," Zoe said. "I figured you sleep in them."

"Exactly."

"Okay, so don't marry him," Zoe suggested. "Do what Josephina Greenberg did. Just have the baby. Don't get married."

"I just don't know if Eamon will understand that. I think I'm just worried about telling him in general. But I have to, like stat. I mean I make sure we have sex in the dark and or he'll see how fat I've gotten."

"I think you just have to do it . . . just lay it on him," Zoe said. "Like the longer you wait, the harder it'll be."

Linda pressed her lips together and nodded. Zoe felt strange being the one in the position to give advice.

"You're right," Linda said.

"Whatever happens, you'll be okay," Zoe said. "You're you. You've totally got this."

Chapter 23

LATER THAT DAY, John and Zoe met Brett in the spectator tent to work out the details of the purchase. Brett had a table in the tent and they sat down with the necessary bank routing and USEF numbers.

The $30,000 Jumper Classic was going on in the grand prix ring. Zoe had checked online and had seen that Morgan was doing it. She kept looking to see who was at the in-gate and spotted him waiting on deck. She let herself glance over a few times when he was in the ring and catch a few jumps.

She couldn't help but wish that he'd crash or at least have a bunch of rails down. From a distance, he looked so completely normal. But of course no normal guy could ever be interested in her. It had to be all the messed up ones that went after her, and that to be honest, she seemed to gravitate toward. All except for John and look how that had worked out.

Of course he went clear. All his horses were top notch, bought from European riders who'd brought them along but couldn't afford to keep them, and his trainer was a former Olympian.

Morgan would never have any horses with quirks. None that had sensitive mouths or could be so careful that they could easily lose their confidence. All his horses were straight-forward and simple to ride. They weren't the kind of horses that you needed to get to know, or build a relationship with. They needed minimal preparation—just flatwork, fitness, and basic jump-schools by Morgan's trainer, and then Morgan could just hop on at the show, go out, and win.

After his ride, Morgan came into the tent, his helmet under the crook of his arm, his hair appealingly sweaty.

Zoe glanced up at him as he passed. He locked eyes with her for a few beats too long, something more than just ac-knowledgement passing between them.

Zoe quickly looked away, her skin flushing red. She could feel John staring at her. He had watched the whole interac-tion. When John caught her eye across the table, he mouthed, "Old friend?"

* * *

By the time the announcer called it a wrap for the day in all rings, Zoe's shoulder throbbed with pain. But what hurt more was facing John when he confronted her back in the barn when she was taking out Gidget's braids.

"He did that to you?" John said. "That guy, Morgan Cleary?"

Zoe didn't know how to answer. She didn't want to admit what had happened. She stayed focused on the braids. There was something terribly satisfying about using a seam ripper to cut the yarn. You wouldn't think it would feel good to basically ruin what was a gorgeous braiding job but there was pleasure in getting the blade of the seam ripper positioned just so underneath the yarn looped around the braid, and then slicing one clean, sharp cut.

"Come on," John said. "I put two and two together. It wasn't hard to figure out. What I can't figure out is why a girl like you, who has so much going for you, would let someone treat you like that?"

"I have so much going for me?" Zoe said. "Please."

John counted off on his fingers. "You're smart, you're an amazing rider, you're a hard worker, you're resilient. You shouldn't be with guys like that."

"I made a mistake," Zoe said. She'd done half of Gidget's mane and the braids were slowly springing loose. Zoe ran her fingers through them, one by one, raking the hair free.

"A big mistake," John said.

Zoe felt a flush of shame. "So now you probably think I'm pathetic."

"No, I think you can do better."

Zoe started in on the remaining braids. If he thought she could do better, than why wasn't she good enough for him?

John collected a dirty saddle pad and two dirty polo wraps and went to put them in the bag to take to the horse laundry place.

"How's your shoulder?"

"It's fine."

"No, it's not. You shouldn't even be doing that. Let me take out the rest—"

"No, it's my left arm. I'm fine," she protested.

"Get off the step-ladder," he said.

Zoe climbed down from the step-ladder and begrudgingly turned the seam ripper over to John. She acted annoyed but inside she was touched that he cared about her.

"You should ice it when you get back to the hotel. I talked to the front desk this morning. Good news. They had a room open up so I'll move when I get back tonight."

"Oh," Zoe said, pretending to be happy. "That's great."

"You promise to ice it?"

"Promise."

* * *

The weather during the second week was erratic. Wednesday the show was ensconced in fog. Zoe was on her first ride of the day at 5:30 since Dakota had a full day of showing between the junior hunters, junior jumpers, and the Washington and Talent Search. Zoe also had Gidget to do in the high performance hunters.

When the show got underway it was hard to believe the judges would even be able to see the jumps with all the fog. By midday the fog had finally worn off but the wind set in, making it feel ten degrees colder. Out again came the down jackets and scarves, the coolers and Burberry plaid dog-blankets. But it was the kind of cold that sunk into your bones and wouldn't let go no matter how many layers you put on.

The wind wreaked havoc with the courses, blowing over standards, bushes, and taking down rails. Any dreams of dozing lazily in chairs by the side of the ring faded fast for the jump crew.

When the day finally came to an end, Zoe couldn't wait to get into her car and out of the wind. But the cold feeling in her bones wouldn't leave until she stood in the shower, the dial turned almost all the way to the red H, letting the water rush over her and turn her skin red.

A hot shower had never felt so good.

Sometime after midnight, the rain started. By the time Zoe was due to get up the next morning, it was darker than dark and the rain was coming down in sheets. At the show everyone dug trenches and then huddled in the tents watching lightning flash across the mountains.

The show was postponed and finally canceled for the day.

It wouldn't be Lake Placid without one day of torrential rain.

Everyone went back to their hotels to catch up on sleep and paperwork.

Before she left, Linda took Zoe aside and said, "This is it. I'm telling him. This afternoon."

"Good luck," Zoe said, but then felt strange for wishing her luck.

The sun was out the next day, bright and promising. Zoe got to the barn before Linda and was out on Plato when Linda arrived. Zoe had wanted to text Linda the night before but she'd felt it was too intrusive. She wanted to wait until she saw her in person.

As she rode up to the barn, she saw Linda in the tack room and tried to read her body language for a sign. She couldn't see anything different in the way she moved about, opening a tack trunk and pulling out a bridle.

Fernando took Plato and she sat down on one of the tack trunks.

"So?" Zoe said.

"So," Linda said coyly.

Zoe slapped her thighs. "You're keeping me in total suspense here . . . did you tell him?"

"I did," Linda said.

"And?"

"He was a little surprised at first. But he said he's always wanted to be a Da. That's what he said—a Da. I guess that's Irish for dad. It was really kind of cute."

"So he didn't talk about . . ." Zoe didn't want to say the word abortion but Linda knew what she meant and it was too late for that by now anyway.

"No, not even for a second."

"And getting married?"

"I told him right away I didn't expect anything from him and I certainly didn't expect us to get married. I told him we could go our separate ways and I'd be fine with that . . . which of course was pretty much a lie."

"What did he say?"

"He said he didn't want that. He wants to stay together. I mean he was pretty shocked. I think he needs to let it sink in, and I don't blame him."

"But overall he was great about it?"

"Super great. And happy too, even though he was still getting used to the idea." Linda smiled. "It's such a relief that he knows."

"What's the big news?"

Zoe and Linda both turned to John, who had come into the tack room.

"Whoa," John said, seeing their faces. "What did I just walk in on?"

"You might as well know," Linda said. "It's not a secret anymore although I guess if we can keep it kind of quiet for a few more days while Eamon wraps his brain around it. I'm pregnant."

"Congratulations!" John said without hesitation.

Zoe loved him for how he didn't say something like, "Really?" Or, "Wow," or "What are you going to do about it?"

Linda looked a little surprised at his positive reaction and John followed up with, "That's happy news, right?"

"Yes," Linda said with growing confidence. "It's very happy news.

Chapter 24

DAKOTA RODE IN THE Kathy Scholl and put in great trips. It was like everything was coming together for her and Plato in the equitation. She ended up third in the very competitive class.

Each day Zoe's shoulder felt better and she tried to put what happened with Morgan behind her.

The derby had a trot jump and Gidget still won it—a huge win for her. Proof that she belonged in the best company.

By all accounts Lake Placid had been a huge success for John's business. He had sold Cruz. Gidget had won the big derby. Dibs had gone well and gotten low ribbons in the pre greens. Dakota had a good show too—she'd ended up qualifying for the Talent Search and had gotten good ribbons in the hunters and jumpers.

On the drive home, Zoe heard the DJ on the radio talking about a Taylor Swift concert coming up at the Met Life Stadium in New Jersey. A thought took shape in her brain before she could even name it. She turned up the volume.

"You know you want to go to this concert," the DJ said.

"This is *the* concert of the summer and it's all sold out but you can still win your tickets here . . ."

Zoe knew she had to take Molly. Molly would be out of her mind excited to see Taylor live.

But how could Zoe pull it off if the shows were already all sold out?

Perhaps Morgan knew someone. Didn't owners of teams have relationships with other teams? Surely he'd be able to help her get two measly tickets. After how he'd hurt her, he owed her.

Zoe called him immediately. *Please answer*, she thought with each ring that passed. But of course he didn't pick up. Maybe he wasn't near his phone or was doing something important. But what could be so important on a Sunday afternoon? He was probably ignoring the call.

She got off at the next exit so she could text him.

I really want to get tickets to Taylor Swift at Met Life Stadium for one of the girls I work with at the therapeutic riding center.

She stopped mid-composition to realize Morgan didn't know the first thing about Narrow Lane. He knew next to nothing about her life.

She rewrote the text.

Really want to get 2 tix to Taylor Swift at Met Life for a friend who's had a hard time. Would mean the world to her. Can u help? Tell you more later. Call me.

Of course he didn't call her back on Sunday, or Monday either. By Tuesday afternoon, she texted him again: *Did you get my text about the Taylor Swift concert?*

Finally, he wrote back: *Can't get concert tix.*

Okay, she answered him. *Thanks for checking.*

But had he really checked? Had he asked around, or even bothered to call her back and hear more about Molly? No. He just didn't care.

Thanks for nothing, is what she should have written.

Asshole.

She flipped her phone around in her hand and thought about how else she could get tickets. There were ticket re-sellers that had tickets to every concert and sporting event imaginable. There was also the radio station contest, but did anyone ever win those?

Some people had to.

Zoe spent the next few hours coasting from one pop station to another on the Morada Bay radio and looking on their websites for information about Taylor Swift ticket giveaways. Two stations were having contests. It was the usual—hear a certain Taylor Swift song on the radio and be caller number whatever.

Well, Zoe would try it.

She felt a surge of excitement and optimism. If she dedicated herself to these contests, maybe she'd actually win. She kept imagining telling Molly—how happy she'd be.

Zoe listened to the stations non-stop for the next few days, whenever she wasn't riding. She listened in the car, with the phone number for the station programmed into her phone.

Three times she heard the Taylor Swift song and was able to call in. Two of those times she got nothing but a busy signal.

On the third time, it finally rang. *This is it*, she thought. *Please, be the right caller*, she chanted in her head. If anyone deserved the tickets, it was Molly, and Zoe had to believe that would count for something—that if there was any karma in the world it would flow her way and she would be the right caller.

"KISS 106," a voice said.

Before Zoe could get out, "Am I the right caller?" the person answering the phone said, "We've already got a winner. Better luck next time."

Better luck next time. Zoe's shoulders dropped as she realized how pointless this was, and how pathetic she was for actually thinking she might be able to win the tickets on the radio.

That evening, she surfed Craigslist for tickets. There were several listings but she'd had a friend who'd gotten tickets off Craigslist and gone to the concert only to find out her tickets were fakes.

She decided not to risk it and called a ticket reseller she found online, Ticket Pronto.

"Do you have Taylor Swift tickets?" she asked.

"Of course we do. How many do you need and what section?"

"Two tickets. What section do you have? I guess something good."

Molly was worth it, she thought, and she did have the money from the commission on Cruz. She could afford to spend a little of that on Molly.

"Section F, Row 15. We've got two."

"How much are those?"

"Those are 1500."

Zoe swallowed hard. "For both? I mean, apiece or to-gether?" Did it matter? Either price was ridiculous.

"Apiece."

"Three thousand dollars? Well, what do you have for less? Like for crappy seats?"

"We have upper balcony for 800 each."

"Eight hundred each?" It was still completely outrageous.

"It's a sold-out show. It's Taylor Swift."

Zoe felt like an idiot. She wasn't some grandma who was trying to get tickets for her granddaughter's birthday. She knew tickets cost a lot and she knew how popular Taylor Swift was.

Zoe ran through a mental list of her expenses, bills she needed to pay off, including the balance on her credit card. She didn't have 1600 dollars to blow on Taylor Swift.

But she kept seeing Molly's face. It would mean everything to her.

Zoe desperately wanted to give Molly that kind of happiness.

"I'll take the balcony seats," she said.

Chapter 25

ZOE COULDN'T WAIT to see the look on Molly's face. When Joanne pulled up in the mini-van, Zoe was there to meet them in the parking lot. "I've got a surprise for Molly," she whispered to Joanne. "I think she's going to be out of her mind excited!"

Joanne paused before opening the sliding door. "Do you want to tell me first?" she asked with a hint of trepidation.

"No, that's okay. It'll be a surprise for you too."

It was nearly impossible for Zoe to keep the news of the tickets to herself for most of Molly's lesson, but she had a big reveal planned. She'd asked Kirsten if they could do the singers on the wall game again and this time she slipped the two tickets into the plastic sleeve that held Taylor's Swift's head shot.

Kirsten wasn't in on the plan—she didn't know yet about the concert. Zoe almost couldn't contain her excitement as Kirsten asked Molly to find Beyoncé and Kelly Clarkson. Finally, Kirsten said, "Okay, Molly, I don't even need to say her name . . ."

"Taylor," Molly said.

The girl was happy just at the sound of the singer's name. She was overjoyed just by having to find her likeness on a wall of the arena.

Zoe's whole body throbbed with her own heartbeat as she waited for Molly to find the tickets. She couldn't remember being so excited to give someone something.

Molly reached the photograph and pulled it off the wall. "There's something in here."

"Take a look," Zoe said, rocking on her toes. "What is it?"

Molly held the plastic close to her face. When she seemed slow to process what the sleeve held Zoe blurted out, "It's two tickets to see Taylor Swift in concert! I'm taking you! I got us tickets!"

Molly let go of the reins, her hands flying to her face. Noises came from her but they weren't words. They were more like a combination of squeaks and sharp breaths. Finally, she calmed down enough to take her hands away from her face. Tears streamed down her cheeks.

"We're going to Taylor Swift?"

"Yes!" Zoe bounced up and down. "We're going! We're going!"

Zoe looked at Kirsten to see her response. Kirsten was smiling but she didn't look as blown away and enthusiastic as Zoe had expected her to.

"I can't even ride anymore," Molly said. "I can't. I'm so excited."

"Me too," Zoe said.

"We can finish up here for today," Kirsten said, all business again.

Zoe led Daisy back to the mounting block.

Kirsten said, "Pat your horse and thank her for the ride."

Joanne was just coming back in and noticed the commotion and the look on Zoe and Molly's faces. "What's up?"

"Mom!" Molly said. "Zoe got me and her tickets to Taylor Swift! I'm going to Taylor Swift!"

Zoe had seen plenty of horse-show-mothers trying to remain calm when they were anything but, and that was exactly what Joanne was doing. Usually this happened at the ring when their supposedly unbelievably talented daughter flubbed a big class. The mother would be trying so hard not to burst into tears or fly into a rage that her face would be arranged in a frozen half-smile. That was how Joanne looked now.

"I hope it's okay I got the tickets," Zoe said.

She tried to imagine what was going through Joanne's mind—what could she be concerned about?

A late night? Zoe's driving? Drunk people at the concert saying rude things about Molly's disability? It was Taylor Swift, not some raucous country band where everyone in the crowd was plastered.

"It was a really nice thought," Joanne said.

A nice thought.

Nice thoughts were actually bad ideas in mom-speak.

Maybe Molly needed certain medication. But couldn't Zoe give it to her? What about her car? Zoe hadn't thought of that, which she realized now was stupid. But couldn't she borrow the minivan? She looked over at Molly's happy, hopeful face.

Joanne got Molly loaded in the minivan, the whole time maintaining her remain-calm expression. Molly kept babbling about the concert, which didn't help the terrible pit growing in Zoe's stomach.

"I wonder what songs she'll play? Will she play her new stuff? She usually has special guests too . . . who could she have this time? Maybe it'll be someone amazing like Joe Jonas."

When the minivan door had slid shut, Joanne led Zoe a few feet away. Zoe bit her lip, waiting for the verdict.

"She can't go to a concert," Joanne said flatly. "Don't you think if she could go to a concert I would have already taken her to see Taylor Swift five hundred times?"

"Why can't she?" Zoe said, somewhat timidly. She followed up with, "I'm so sorry. I just don't understand."

"Because she can't walk into a huge stadium, go up stairs, sit in a hard-backed seat for what would be five hours by the time the opening acts play and they finally get to Taylor Swift."

"Couldn't we just show up late, like right before Taylor comes on?"

"When the stadium is packed full of people screaming and talking and singing? You're going to walk in with Molly . . . *You* are going to stand behind Molly and walk her in? She can barely walk over well-lit, even ground and it'll be dark with people's spilled drinks and feet to trip over. It's asking for an accident."

"I thought maybe she could use a wheelchair. I guess we'd have to use your van. Maybe you could drive us? I didn't think through all the details."

"No, you didn't. Did you get handicapped accessible seats?"

Of course she didn't. Zoe pressed her fingers to the bottom of her eyelids, trying not to cry. Molly was so happy and excited. Now she'd be crushed.

"Look," Joanne said. "I know you meant well. You like Molly and that's so nice for her."

"I do," Zoe said. "I really like her so much."

"I know, and you probably think I'm being overprotective and a kill-joy but you don't know anything about what it's like to manage her condition. She has a bad fall or gets a common cold and things can go south frighteningly fast. Her body is not like other people's bodies and it's not just what you see on the outside. It's on the inside too. I *am* being overprotective because I have to be. Because her body can't protect itself."

"I get it," Zoe said. "I'm so sorry. I made such a mess of all this. She's going to be crushed."

They were silent for a moment, each likely imagining the same thing: telling Molly there would be no concert.

"I'll tell her," Zoe said. "It was my stupid idea and I'll tell her I didn't think it through enough and it's my fault. You shouldn't be the one to have to tell her."

"I've told her harder things before," Joanne said.

Zoe nodded and walked back into Narrow Lane in a daze.

"Are you okay?" Kirsten said.

"She can't go," Zoe said despondently.

Kirsten closed her eyes briefly like she had already known the outcome.

"I hate that I did that to her," Zoe said.

"I know you do but these kids are tough. People look at them and think they're fragile but they're tough."

Kirsten was being kind but she wasn't really making Zoe feel better.

"By the way, I wanted to let you know you've completed all your required hours."

"Does that mean you want me to stop working here? Is this about what just happened—"

"No," Kirsten rushed to reassure her. "I just wanted you to know."

"I like being here," Zoe said, tears flooding her eyes.

"Then keep coming," Kirsten said, looking at her earnestly. "Okay? We like having you here."

"You sure?" Zoe asked.

"Yes," Kirsten said emphatically.

* * *

For the rest of the day Zoe was sick to her stomach about setting Molly up and then letting her down. She should have known better. She should have asked Joanne or John first about the concert. But none of the details Joanne pointed out had even occurred to her.

She'd been so intoxicated with the idea and now she'd blown her whole commission on a concert she wasn't going to go to. She couldn't go without Molly. That would feel all wrong. And it wasn't even about the money. It was about Molly. Zoe kept seeing her face when she'd found the tickets in the plastic sleeve.

It was just like Zoe to rush into doing something without thinking. When would she ever learn?

And now John would undoubtedly heap on the disapproval as well.

When she drove into his farm that afternoon, she spotted him on the riding mower out in one of the fields between the barn and the house. He had ear protectors on and a straw hat and there was something incredibly sexy about seeing him out there. It was just the emotion she didn't need to feel right now—attraction. It felt out of place, like laughing at a funeral.

She went ahead and brought Gidget out. She brushed her off and was putting on her front boots when John came into the barn. He was sweaty from being out in the sun, his neck red.

"Have you talked to your mother?" she said immediately.

"No, is something wrong?" His face looked panicked, as if something terrible had happened to Molly while he was out on the mower.

"No, nothing's wrong. I mean your mom's fine, Molly's fine." Zoe saw relief on his face. "But I fucked up royally."

"How?"

Zoe was still holding the front boots that she hadn't put on yet. She told John about the tickets, starting with how she had heard about the concert and thought Molly would love it.

She could tell he had a sense for how the story would end as he started to grimace nearly the moment he heard her say, "Tickets to Taylor Swift."

When she was done explaining what had happened, he said, "Poor Molly."

"And stupid, asshole me."

"You tried to do something nice. Your intent was good."

"But that's what always happens with me. My intent seems good and then what I end up doing is a big pile of dog shit."

"Okay, it's not the end of the world."

"You should've seen her face when she saw the tickets . . ."

"I can imagine."

"Now your mom totally hates me."

"I doubt that."

"No, she does. I'm sure of it. I want to do something to make it up to Molly but I don't know what to do."

"Just come over tonight," John said. "She just wants to be around you. She likes you. She likes having a friend. Honestly, it's that simple with her. She doesn't need Taylor Swift tickets."

"But she would have loved it . . ." Zoe said, wistful. "And your mother definitely doesn't want me coming over. She probably never wants to see me again."

"My mom's pretty forgiving," John said. "One time I cut up her favorite sweater to make my own custom fuzzies for a halter."

"Seriously?" Zoe said.

"Yes, and she forgave me and took me to the tack store to buy real fuzzies."

Thinking of John as a young boy, cutting up his mother's sweater into fuzzies made Zoe smile.

John nodded to the boots in Zoe's hands. "Finish tacking up. I'll get on Oakley and meet you out there."

* * *

It killed Zoe that Molly didn't even seem that upset when she came over that night. Zoe noticed a look in Molly's eyes, a look that told Zoe Molly had been down this road before. That disappointment was a big part of life for her.

"It's okay," Molly told her. "I think she's probably better to listen to at home than in a concert anyway with all the other people there yelling."

"I'm so sorry," Zoe said.

"It's okay," Molly said. "Really."

"Do you still want to watch a movie tonight?" Zoe asked.

"I was thinking maybe *The Spectacular Now*," Molly said.

"Yeah," Zoe said. "That's perfect."

Chapter 26

DAKOTA WAS ACTING weird around Zoe. Instead of being her talkative self, she was quiet and distanced. She said a curt hello and then carefully avoided looking at her.

When Zoe said, "What's up?" she replied, "Nothing much," and walked on.

Dakota stared at her phone so she wouldn't have to talk to Zoe and when they rode together she seemed to make a point of never looking at her and even cutting across the ring or circling so they wouldn't have to pass.

"What's going on with her?" Zoe asked Linda.

"I don't know. Maybe something with her parents? They haven't been home all summer."

Zoe decided to make Dakota talk to her when she was waiting for Angelique to pick her up and take her back into the city.

"Okay, cut the bullshit, what the hell is going on with you?" Zoe said.

Dakota still didn't look up from her phone. "I should be asking you the same thing."

"Huh?" Zoe said. "I'm not the one being standoffish."

Dakota finally looked up for long enough to shoot Zoe a cold look. "No, you're the one being all slutty and stupid."

Zoe swallowed, caught off guard. She took a moment to process that Dakota probably knew about Morgan. If that was the case, Dakota was right to call her out. Zoe had hoped she could put the night in Lake Placid with Morgan behind her but she should have known it wouldn't be that easy to wipe it from existence.

"You're talking about Morgan Cleary?" she said, just to confirm. You never knew what gossip could be circulating.

"Yup," Dakota said.

"I made a mistake," she said. "I would think maybe you could understand. I mean it wasn't like he was just anyone. He's Morgan Cleary."

Dakota positioned a hand on her hip. "What's that supposed to mean?"

"He's a billionaire," Zoe pointed out.

"So it's okay to go out with assholes if they have lots of money? Oh, that's good for me to know going forward. So then we need to amend our pact. No dating assholes unless they have money. You are a really great role model."

Zoe hated Dakota's sarcastic tone. And it was different for her. Dakota would never have to worry about money. "You have money of your own," Zoe said. "You don't have any idea what it's like to be broke-ass-poor and have credit card debts up to your eye-balls."

"I'd rather be broke-ass-poor than be with an asshole. When we made the pact I thought I was the one who'd have to work hard not to break it. You were supposed to be the adult."

"You don't know me very well at all then," Zoe said. "I never act like an adult." She wanted to point out that if she had gone to college like most nineteen year-olds she'd hardly be considered an adult. It was only in the horse world that crossing the monumental age eighteen made you suddenly adult.

Dakota flipped her phone in its Vineyard Vines case in her hand. "I thought you'd changed. I thought you'd grown up."

Zoe didn't know what to say back. She'd thought she'd changed too, and grown up some. And maybe she had but that didn't mean she got it all right. It had been tempting to think that being with Morgan might solve all her problems.

Still, she shouldn't have broken her promise to Dakota. It killed her that Dakota actually believed in her and saw her as a mature, big-sister-like figure. It killed her that she'd let her down. It was the second time in days she'd let someone down. And Dakota probably didn't even have any idea of how Morgan had hurt her. If she knew that, then what would she think?

"Okay, so I blew it. Let's try again. We'll start the pact over again."

"No," Dakota said sharply. "It's over. It's done. You already killed it."

"So that's it? You're going to go out with whoever now just because I messed up?"

Dakota squinted at her. "I didn't say that. Just because you don't care about yourself doesn't mean I'm going to do something stupid too."

Zoe didn't point out that Dakota was not exactly known for her clear head. "Well, that's good to hear. I'm glad you're smarter than me. I'm glad you're not going to make all the same fucked up mistakes I do. Don't, okay?"

"Don't tell me what to do," Dakota said.

Angelique pulled up and Dakota ran to the car and jumped in, without even looking back at Zoe.

Linda must have caught some of what had just gone on between them because when Zoe walked back into the barn she said, "What was that all about?"

"We had kind of an agreement. Like we made a promise to each other that we wouldn't go out with assholes. She found out about me being with Morgan in Lake Placid. Not about my shoulder—thank God—or at least I don't think she knows about that but just that I hooked up with him. It was probably on HorseShowDrama."

"So she's pissed you broke your promise?"

"Yup, and she deserves to be." Zoe looked at the ground, embarrassed. It was bad enough that her actions hurt herself; worse that they had hurt others. "That girl has no one in her life to look up to and I guess I thought for a deluded moment maybe I could be that person."

"I'd like to think she can look up to me too," Linda said. "But then I guess there's the whole knocked-up unmarried thing."

Dakota had seemed excited when Linda had told her she was pregnant. Maybe she'd always wanted a sibling and this was the closest she'd get to it.

The Pearces had been overwhelmingly positive too. They said they knew she'd be able to work out having a baby and still training Dakota.

"They don't believe in parents actually raising their children," Linda had joked to Zoe. "I'm sure they think I've already got my live-in hired."

Zoe stole a glance at Linda's cute baby bump. There was no disguising her pregnancy now.

"She can totally look up to you, even when she knows you got yourself knocked-up," Zoe said. "I guess I just liked the idea of her looking up to me."

"So what's the deal with you and Morgan anyway?"

Behind them in one of the stalls, a horse sneezed. Another—undoubtedly it was the ever cocky Plato—banged his door demanding his afternoon flake of hay.

"Nothing. It's over. I knew I wasn't anything to him but I guess I couldn't help but think it could change into something real."

"It's not going to," Linda said.

"I know. Why did he even bother with me? Given who he is, why does he want to risk having his name all over Horse-ShowDrama?"

"You're his big rebellion. His one last fuck-you to his family before he takes over the company and marries some little miss priss."

"Like Julia."

Linda nodded.

"He's a deeply unhappy man," Zoe said.

"They all are, hon."

"Not all of them. Not Eamon."

"Not Eamon. And not John," Linda said, her eyebrows raised.

Chapter 27

VERMONT WAS PERHAPS the closest thing to home for Zoe. If she counted up the weeks she spent in one place horse-showing, Wellington would by far have the most weeks but it was hard to feel like Wellington was home for her, even though many people made Wellington their home base. And maybe someday she'd decide to make it hers. But WEF was too crazy-busy, too frenetic to feel like home.

The Vermont Circuit was quieter, nestled in a small village with a picture-postcard mountain backdrop. Jamie had always taken her barn to Vermont so Zoe had been coming since she showed in the ponies. It was true that she'd had some pretty wild times there and not all her memories were happy ones but there was a certain comfort to the warm days and the cool nights, the clean air, and the sight of tractors parked next to old farmhouses.

The professional divisions were light at Vermont—it was the children's and adult classes that were chock-a-block full.

There was no horse that could even come close to giving

Gidget a run for the blue in the high performance workings. Zoe picked up two saddle pads, a halter, a scrim sheet, and a gift certificate for a bridle for winning nearly every class in the division.

Zoe won the derbies both weeks too. There was a little more competition in those but Gidget still rose to the top. She had talent and now she and Zoe were building confidence in each other.

The second week they were there, Callie caught her walking back from her morning hack on Gidget. "Did you hear about Lindsay?"

"No, what?"

"She fell off a greenie and shattered her femur."

"Oh no," Zoe said, trying to camouflage the small dash of hope she felt fluttering inside her chest.

It never felt good to take pleasure in other people's misfortune but on the show circuit that was pretty much routine. If you were a grand prix rider, you hoped for horses to drop rails; if you were a hunter rider, you wished for horses to spook or be late with a change.

Generally you didn't actually wish harm on a horse or rider but in this case an injury to a top hunter rider meant a possible job opening for Zoe.

"Yeah. She'll be out months. She's got pins inserted and everything."

Lindsay had a unicorn job in the horse show world. Not a job riding unicorns, but a job that was hard to find. She rode exclusively for a wealthy woman who had been around the show circuit forever.

Kathleen had been a good junior rider. Then, because of her ability to buy expensive horses, she'd become one of the best amateur riders and had won nearly everything there was to win in the hunters. Championships at every major horse show from Devon to The National. She'd dabbled in the jumpers for a time but going fast and jumping high wasn't really for her.

Her first marriage to a professional hadn't lasted long. In her forties, she married a Wall Street type and, after many attempts at IVF, finally had a son.

She'd ridden off and on since becoming a mother, but lately had transitioned to owning horses that showed in the professional divisions. Among her talented horses was Three Wishes. He'd won the derbies in Wellington, Devon, Tryon, and Upperville, to name a few.

She'd bought a gorgeous farm in Lexington and her horses spent summers there and winters in Wellington.

Her trainer since her junior years was Grant Day. Now in his sixties, he'd once been the best hunter rider in the country. One knee and two hip replacements later, Grant just flatted the horses. Lindsay showed them.

"Who's going to get the ride on all her horses?" Zoe asked.

Callie shrugged. "Someone said Jeremy."

Jeremy was a versatile rider, having ridden on Nations Cup teams and won plenty in the hunters too. He wouldn't be a bad choice but Zoe could think of only one person who would be perfect: herself.

It was all she thought about the rest of the day. Should she call Grant and offer her services? Should she text him to say she was sorry to hear about Lindsay and that way she'd be in the forefront of his mind, or should she tell him she was available if he needed her?

Should she text Lindsay and maybe that would get back to Grant? Lindsay suggesting her might be the best option. She decided to do that.

If there's anything I can do lmk.

Sucks, Lindsay texted back. *But I heal quickly.*

After that exchange, Zoe waited and waited, hoping she'd hear from either Lindsay or Grant.

Finally, three days later, she saw Grant's number on her Caller ID. "Hi, there," she said, trying to act casual. "So sorry to hear about Lindsay."

"I know. Real bad timing but what'cha gonna do? That's life with horses."

"That's a good way to look at it," she said. Her heart was pounding. *Just ask me,* she thought. *Just please.*

There was no way he was calling for any other reason.

"So listen, I need a rider for my horses for Derby Finals," he said. "You interested?"

She swallowed, trying to give herself a moment so she didn't respond too quickly, but it was no use.

"Hells yeah!"

"Great," Grant said. "I think you'll be perfect with them."

"Did Lindsay suggest me?" Zoe asked.

"Yeah, we were throwing names around once Jeremy said he couldn't do it. A lot of people are booked up."

Zoe wanted to kick herself for asking. If she hadn't asked, she wouldn't know that she wasn't their first choice or maybe even their second or third. But it didn't matter, she told herself. She'd ride the shit out of those horses and come in first, second, and third. Then she'd be everyone's top choice.

"When can you get down here?" Grant said. "We need you right away. I'm going to have you riding all the horses. I'll pay you good money so don't worry about that, and we'll put you up. I could use you straight through to Florida if things go well."

"Um, yeah, I just gotta take care of some things up here first. But I can get down there super fast, I'm sure."

"You're not committed to whoever you're riding for, are you?" Grant asked. "No one seemed to think you were."

"No, no. I'm not. But I just can't up and leave, like today."

"Of course, take a few days," Grant said, like that was being generous. "Text me when you're on your way."

"Okay," Zoe said. "Great. Thanks."

"Sure thing, hon."

Zoe pressed end. She should have been ecstatic, but her initial excitement at getting what she'd thought she wanted had turned to unease.

How the hell was she going to tell John and Linda she was leaving?

Chapter 28

THIS WAS THE CHANCE she'd been waiting for. This was the call-up to the major leagues. John would have to understand that. And Linda too.

Wouldn't they?

So why was she so far seemingly incapable of telling them? One day passed and then another. She could never find the right moment.

Her secret became unbearable when John started asking her about plans for Kentucky and Derby Finals. When should they leave? How many days before the derby should they get there? What classes, if any, would they plan to do with Gidget before the derby?

Yet she still couldn't bring herself to tell him.

She began to think about just getting in her car and leaving and then texting him and Linda from the road. She knew it would be so wrong, like breaking up with someone over text, but it would be easier that way.

She'd tell him that of course she'd still ride Gidget in

Derby Finals. John could keep Gidget in shape and bring her down to Kentucky. Grant hadn't said anything about her only riding his horses in the final.

Zoe still hadn't told John when he came back to the tent with his jaw set. She hadn't really ever seen him angry before but she could still tell this was high-level pissed off.

"What the hell?" he said. "You weren't even going to tell me?"

"About Grant's horses?" she said.

"Yes, about Grant's horses."

"Who told you?"

"What does it matter?"

"I can still ride Gidget," she said.

"You think I still want you to ride my mare?"

Suddenly it was *my mare*.

"I guess I thought you would, yeah."

"You have no idea how the real world works," John said. "You may be the most gifted hunter rider I've ever seen but you need some lessons on how to treat people and how to treat yourself too."

"What, I'm not supposed to take this job? Take this opportunity? Do you know how amazing his horses are? I could be first, second, and third at Derby Finals. Seriously, I could."

Zoe knew she sounded arrogant but she wanted to make John understand she couldn't pass this up.

"I never said you're not supposed to take this job." John raised his hands and shook them at her, as if he needed to demonstrate just how frustrated he was. "But you're supposed to talk to me about it. We have a partnership going.

Maybe we didn't put it in writing but we were just talking about plans for Kentucky, and you didn't say anything. You lied to me."

"I didn't lie. I just—"

"Please—" John said, stopping her.

"I didn't know how to tell you. I was trying to figure it out. Would you have said I should take the job?"

"I would have asked you what you thought about it, about what you wanted to do. We would have talked about it. That's what grown people do."

Grown people did not take off and text, which Zoe felt certain she would have done if John hadn't found out.

"Can we talk about it now?" she tried.

"What's there to talk about? You've already made up your mind. When are you leaving?"

Zoe grimaced. "Um, like in the next few days."

"You're serious?"

"He needs me to start riding."

"Okay, great," John said. "Then apparently everything's all set."

"Wait, but do you still want me to ride Gidget at Derby Finals if I can?"

John was pensive for a moment. He stared at the ground and only after a few beats raised his eyes to look at her again. "No, I don't want you to ride her."

"Are you going to ride her?"

"What do you care?"

"I think she's a great horse and it would be a shame if she didn't show at Derby Finals."

"I think you should just get in your car and take off right now. Why wait a few days to leave? What I do with my horses has nothing to do with you anymore."

"Don't you think you're overreacting a little?" Zoe said. "I mean, I'm riding his horses for a few months. It's not like we can't have anything to do with each other ever again."

"It's how you went about it. You apparently aren't capable of thinking things through, or considering other people's lives besides your own. And sometimes you're pretty downright shitty about that too."

Zoe knew she'd done things the wrong way but it felt like John was being a little too harsh.

She narrowed her eyes. "Did you ever think maybe you have a little problem? Did you ever think maybe there's another reason why you never got further as a junior than your parents not having tons of money or your sister's CP?

"Maybe you're scared of putting yourself out there? If you wanted to win the Medal Finals so freaking badly you would have found a trainer and done what it took to get rides. That's what the good, hungry kids do. It's easier for you to blame it on the mediocre horse and everyone else using shortcuts. *Oh, I don't use draw reins or over-school my horses . . .*"

Zoe expected a huge reaction but John just shook his head. "Good luck at Derby Finals. I hope you win. And don't forget to tell Linda. And maybe give Molly a call and let her know you won't be at any of her lessons or coming over to watch movies. Or do you want me to tell her for you?"

"I'll tell her," Zoe said. "Maybe I'll see you at Derby

Finals. Or maybe I won't?" She raised her eyebrows, taunting him.

John waved her away with his hand, like she wasn't even worth bothering with, and headed out of the tent.

Zoe didn't cry. She was pissed. Her body was filled with so much anger that she was shaking as she packed up all her stuff from the barn. She threw open tack trunks, grabbing pairs of gloves, sticky spray, hairnets, water bottle, boot-cleaning kit, phone charger; everything that was hers. She dumped it all in her car and texted Linda to find out where she was.

Linda was at the jumper ring. Zoe couldn't handle telling her there and possibly causing a scene so she waited till she came back to the tent. Luckily, John hadn't returned from wherever he'd gone.

"What's up?" Linda said with concern at seeing Zoe's anguished face.

"I don't know if you've heard through the horse show grapevine but you know how Lindsay broke her leg . . ."

"Yeah?"

"Grant called me and asked me to fill in for her, for Derby Finals, and for the next few months."

"Oh, honey, that's quite a compliment to your riding."

"I know. I think I need to take it." Zoe was cringing inside that she'd already accepted the position. John was right, goddamn it. She should have told Grant she needed time to think about things and asked him to at least give her time to help Linda find someone to replace her.

"Definitely," Linda said. "It's a great opportunity for you."

"But what are you going to do?"

"We'll manage," Linda said.

"How?"

"I'm sure John'll ride some for me until I can find some-one, and I'm going to get on the horn and find someone. There are plenty of people out there looking for work. When does Grant need you?"

Zoe gritted her teeth. "As soon as possible."

Linda nodded. She understood how things worked in this business. She didn't expect office protocol of giving two weeks notice in a situation like this, with a big finals coming up.

"I'm so sorry to leave you hanging like this but I don't know what else to do. I can call around and ask some people . . . see if I can get you a good rider."

"I think we both know all the same people," Linda said. Zoe could sense the disappointment in her voice. But at least she wasn't as upset as John. "What about John? Did you tell him yet?"

"Yeah, um, he's bullshit at me."

"Are you still showing Gidget at Derby Finals?"

"He doesn't want me to anymore."

"Wow, he was that upset?"

"He kind of found out from someone else before I had the chance to tell him."

Linda straightened her shirt over her baby bump, pulling it down a little. "That's not good."

"No, it wasn't. I also think there was something between us so that's all mixed up with it."

Linda brightened. "You two? I told you he'd be good for you."

"Nothing happened. Nothing. Like nothing. Which is pretty crazy for me, as you know."

Linda gave a kind of painful smile where she pulled her lips back and pressed her teeth together—half-smile, half-wince. "Maybe that means it was actually real?"

"Well, whatever it was, it's not now. It's done, over."

"Really? You sure?"

Zoe thought about the mega-fight she and John had just had, the mean things they'd said to each other. "Yup, I'm pretty sure."

"Are you sure this is the right thing to do . . . I mean I know Grant's got Three Wishes and all but . . . John's a good guy. This is temporary, whereas something with John . . ."

Linda trailed off but Zoe knew what she meant.

"Even if I wasn't sure about what I was doing, I just burned the bridge with John. In fact, I think I blew up the entire surrounding area near the bridge. Decimated it. And I already told Grant yes and if I renege on that . . ."

"Okay," Linda said. "If your mind's set then come here."

She hugged Zoe tight, rocking slightly back and forth as she did. Zoe didn't want to press too hard for fear of somehow hurting the baby. "I'm sorry to do this to you. Such bad timing."

"Don't worry," she said. "It'll be fine."

Chapter 29

BUT IT DID NOT FEEL fine as she pulled out of the showgrounds. John hadn't spoken to her since their fight. Dakota had barely said good-bye.

"I'm leaving to go ride for Grant Day," she'd told her. "To take over for Lindsay."

"Yeah, Linda told me," Dakota said flatly.

"I know she'll find someone good to replace me, and it's not forever with Grant. I mean maybe I'll be back," she said, even though she doubted it. The point was to use riding for Grant to get her another job riding and showing.

"Great," Dakota said, giving her an unabashedly fake smile. "Drive carefully."

The last person she had to break the news to before she left wasn't a person. It was Gidget. She'd gone around and planted kisses on all the horses first, Logan and Midway and even cocksure Plato.

She found herself in front of Gidget's stall door. The mare had her butt to the door and didn't budge, swing her head, or even flick an ear when Zoe called to her. Zoe opened the door and went to the back of the stall. "That's okay, I'll come to you," she said.

When she was standing in front of her she whispered, "I'm leaving for a while, girlfriend."

Gidget finally glanced at her and then turned away again, flattening her ears.

"You're going places," Zoe told her. "You've got what it takes but you already know that. You've got it all figured out, unlike the rest of us."

Zoe desperately wanted to hug her, to press her cheek against her coat, like she did as a child with all the horses at her mother's farm on those sad, lonely nights.

"I'm doing it—I'm hugging you," she said. "Bite me if you want."

Instead Gidget let out a big sigh.

"See, a little affection isn't so bad." As she left, Gidget actually watched her go. "You just think I have a banana somewhere that I'm not giving you," Zoe said, her voice choking up. She hated leaving Gidget, maybe even more than she hated leaving Linda or John. She also hated leaving Molly, especially without saying good-bye.

"Stop looking at me," Zoe said. "Put your ears back. Look mean." But for once, Gidget wouldn't and it nearly broke Zoe's heart.

It took a few hours to get back to Bedford. Zoe had planned to spend the night, pack up her stuff, and leave early the next morning. But sitting in her sad apartment, she made the impulsive decision to pack up immediately and start driving. She'd drive as far as she could, maybe drive all night. If she got too tired she could find a hotel.

It didn't take her long to pack, which was depressing in itself. Some people had so much stuff, so many things, that they felt weighed down by the clutter. Those people dreamed of purging all the useless stuff, and lightening their load.

But Zoe's life was the opposite. She owned nothing of substance besides her clothes and her two saddles. It felt disheartening to realize your life fit into the back of your car. As she threw her last bag in, she wondered if she'd ever have a house of her own.

Then came the monotonous hours of highway, with quick stops to use disgusting side-of-the-road gas station bathrooms and buy caffeinated beverages and junk snacks. The worst thing when you've got too much on your mind is to be in a car for hours by yourself.

The large green signs that loomed overhead and the minutes slowly passing on the dashboard clock were the only signs of progress. Radio stations came in and out of tune; more country stations cropped up the further south she traveled.

Somewhere along the way, when it wasn't yet too late, she called Hannah and was thrilled when she actually picked up.

"How's Vermont?" Hannah asked.

"I left actually. Grant called me because Lindsay broke her femur and she has pins in it and shit so she's out for months. I'm doing her horses at Derby Finals."

"Three Wishes? You're riding *Three Wishes*?"

"I know, right?"

"That is so awesome," Hannah said. "It's just what you wanted!"

Zoe was quiet on the other end and Hannah added, "Isn't it? What am I missing here?"

"I had to pick up and leave Linda rider-less and John too. Linda understood or she pretended to anyway, but John didn't. And, I don't know, there was something between us. And now he hates me."

"Hates you?"

"I didn't tell him right away and then he found out from someone else that I was leaving."

Hannah made a sucking-in-her-breath sound.

"Yeah," Zoe said. "It got ugly."

"Maybe he'll get over it? Give it time. Plus, this job is only temporary, right? After Lindsay comes back, you'll go back there?"

"I don't know. That's too far off to know, and by that time it'll be Florida and John doesn't go to Florida. I think this is a case of it just not being the right time. You know when that happens, you like someone and maybe he likes you and you could have had something good but the timing just sucks."

"Yeah," Hannah said, rueful. "I know all about that."

Zoe realized she'd been being selfish—only talking about herself. "How's it going there? Are you getting over him?"

"I guess so," Hannah said. "I read somewhere that it takes twice as long as the relationship to get over someone so that means I've got like another year to go."

"If it took twice as long as you dated someone to get over

them, then no one would ever get over anybody," Zoe pointed out.

"Well, I guess you can be with someone else but still not be over your ex."

Zoe sighed. "Oh my God, you're overthinking all of this. This is just like you. Are you going out with friends? Hooking up with anyone?"

"I've been doing the going-out-with-friends part," she said.

"But not the hooking up?"

"I don't think I want to just hook up with someone. Not after what happened with McNair. I'm still recovering from that."

"Water under the bridge," Zoe said. "Trust me. You gotta let that one go."

The distraction of Hannah's problems was helping Zoe feel mildly better. She liked how with Hannah she was the savvy one.

Hannah was quiet for a moment and then said, "Have you heard anything from Chris?"

"I've seen some of the results. Looks like the team is doing well."

"I've seen those too. I meant have you *heard* anything."

Zoe knew what she meant. She meant had she heard anything about whether Chris was back together with Mary Beth. She couldn't blame Hannah for asking. Truthfully, she hadn't heard anything. Morgan would be someone who would know. He was friends with Mary Beth. They ran in the same circles. But she wasn't about to ask him.

"I haven't heard anything."

"Are you just trying to not hurt my feelings because maybe, if I knew he was with her, it would be better for me. Then maybe I could really move on, once and for all."

Zoe switched lanes to pass a motor home with Colorado plates. "I swear I actually don't know anything but maybe I can subtly ask around if you want."

"I don't know what I want," Hannah said. "Maybe it's better if I don't know."

"You haven't texted him or anything?"

"No, I've been good about that. Believe me, I've wanted to. I've liked some of his posts but I figure that's harmless. I keep checking to see what he's listening to on Spotify."

"It'll get easier," Zoe said. "I've been where you were and I promise, it will."

When they finally hung up, Zoe felt all sad inside. Maybe it was just being alone in the car again and having to think about how it had ended with John. A Luke Bryan song came on and it only made her think about him more.

But it was also that she wasn't sure she'd really been where Hannah was now, like she'd told her. Hannah and Chris had been truly, deeply in love. Anyone could have recognized that.

Zoe had never been truly, deeply in love. She'd had crushes, she'd lusted after guys, she'd had hook-ups (many drunken), and she'd had friends-with-benefits.

She'd never found herself falling in love with anyone, till John.

Chapter 30

LYMAN CREEK FARM was everything it should have been. After driving through the night, Zoe pulled through the stately front gate at around six in the evening. Mature trees stood between the winding driveway and the rolling pastures. At a corner of one of the pastures sat a large coop jump—clearly the hunt came through the property. The pastures stretched as far as Zoe could see, meeting the sky where the setting sun cast stripes of pale purple.

Grant had left instructions with the barn manager to send Zoe up to the main house. More dogs than she could count met her at the door. Grant held a crystal highball glass in one hand and a dog in the other.

Here was a man who had mastered the show world. He was one of the few trainers who had job security, and wasn't always depending on his next sale to pay a backload of bills. He had a generous salary, health insurance, and probably even a 401K. He had a long-time boyfriend, a house with nice furniture, and a beautiful farm.

Next to him, Zoe felt like a vagabond.

"You looked exhausted, hon," he said.

"I am," she admitted. "I drove through the night."

"Then you need to get some rest. We'll chat in the mañana."

Zoe nodded, grateful that he apparently knew just what she needed. He had a bit of a fatherly presence and Zoe remembered that before he had come out as gay he'd been married and had a daughter.

She had a suite with a kitchenette in a hotel two exits from the farm. She planned on getting dinner but after a hot shower she lay down on the bed and the next thing she knew it was six the next morning.

She found a morning show on T.V. and listened as she scrolled through her Facebook and Insta feeds. She snapped a pic of her hotel and snapchatted it to Hannah with the text: *My New Home.*

On her way to the barn she found a bagel place and stopped to get breakfast and coffee.

When she drove into the barn, still chewing the last of her bagel, Grant was already on a horse. She parked and walked out to the ring to say hello.

"You look a little more rested," he said, pulling up to a walk. He wasn't a pretty picture on a horse these days. His back was roached and his knees stuck out but he still could train a horse better than many.

He was mostly known as a judge and a trainer now but several decades ago he'd been one of the best hunter riders. Every so often a vintage photo of him made the rounds on the

Equestrians Back in the Day Facebook group and everyone commented on what a gifted rider he'd been.

"I slept like the dead," she said.

"Ready to ride?" he asked.

"You bet."

Zoe rode seven that day. It was more than she'd ridden in a while and the soreness in her legs felt wonderful.

Lindsay, her leg in a full cast, showed up mid-morning after a doctor's appointment, and sat in a golf cart by the ring. She gave Zoe a brief history of all the horses she'd be riding, where they were from, how old they were, how long they'd had them, what they'd been showing in, and how they went best. Zoe didn't know the greenies but the derby horses needed no introduction.

"That's my baby you're on now," Lindsay said when Zoe came out on Three Wishes, or Trey as he was called around the barn.

"I can't believe I get to ride him," Zoe replied.

"Don't get too used to it." She was smiling as she said it but Zoe knew she was serious too. This was her territory. It was one thing for Zoe to help out but Lindsay had a career to protect.

"I won't," Zoe said, trying to put Lindsay at ease. "I'll just enjoy it while I can."

Over the next few weeks, Lindsay watched Zoe when she jumped the horses. Grant was there to supervise too. Kathleen never made an appearance, which Zoe thought was kind of strange until Lindsay told her that her marriage was on the rocks and she was staying up north, trying to work things out.

Lyman Creek was just the type of operation Zoe had longed to be a part of. The horses were high quality. The grooms kept the barn spotless and well-organized. Zoe never had to pick up a pile of manure or sweep the aisle. Not once did anyone ask her to grab a horse from a paddock or throw even one measly flake of hay.

Nearly every day vets, farriers, and other professionals came in and out, providing expert care, and still, there was never one single moment where the staff was shorthanded and could have used Zoe's help.

She should have been feeling ecstatic about working at Lyman Creek but it felt all wrong. She wanted to grab a pitchfork or put a halter on a horse but anytime she tried to offer, or even just stepped in, the grooms popped up out of nowhere and took over.

"No, it's okay, I want to put on his boots," Zoe would say.

But whatever groom was tacking up the horse would shake his head, smiling, and say, "No." He'd keep saying, "No," until she gave in and handed over the boots. Once a groom had to literally pull a broom out of her hands.

She, Lindsay, and Grant worked well together. Maybe it was easy to get along when you had such nice horses. They were well broke and just so talented. Even the green ones were relatively level-headed. With such nice horses you weren't arguing about the best way to fix insurmountable problems and whether you should use nefarious means.

Each night Zoe went to her nice hotel room, and felt like crying. She missed John. She missed Molly. She missed Linda and Dakota and Gidget and Midway. She missed them all. She missed Narrow Lane and leading kids around the ring again and again, and mucking out stalls. She even missed Daisy and Pepper.

She missed trail rides with John and just hanging around the barn with him, getting the horses ridden. She composed texts to him in her head and even typed out a few of them on her phone but always ended up deleting them.

She texted with Linda, who said John still brought Gidget over to her farm for jump-schools. *He always asks about you*, Linda said.

Really?

Always.

She looked back through photos of her and John and Molly. Selfies they'd taken watching movies, and photos Zoe had snapped at Narrow Lane.

There were times when she thought she'd made the worst mistake possible. That she should have stayed with John and Linda. But then she would tell herself that, no, she'd done the right thing. No one would turn down riding Three Wishes at Derby Finals.

This was what she'd wanted ever since she'd ridden her last jump as a junior. This was her chance to get back in the winner's circle.

She wished Lindsay or Grant would invite her for dinner but while they were friendly to her they didn't go the extra mile. So she was left alone in her hotel room, with too much time to think. She thought about Florida and the stealing, replaying some of her darkest moments. She thought about how Dakota felt Zoe had let her down and how she hadn't been able to take Molly to Taylor Swift. She'd sold the tickets back to the ticket place and took a loss on them.

She thought about Brayden and how scared he must have been in the last few minutes before he died.

When Morgan texted to ask her if she'd like to grab a drink, she said yes immediately. She wanted anything to get her out of her own mind and she'd already blown the pact and lost John. What did being with Morgan matter anymore? In fact, maybe she deserved to be treated like shit.

She didn't even know how Morgan knew she was in Lexington, or why he was suddenly there. He'd probably come to do the grand prix at Kentucky Summer II.

All contact she ever had with Morgan had an air of mysteriousness to it, like he paid people to know things about people, like where they were and what they were doing at any given time.

At the bar they went to, she let herself have two drinks and either the bartender had made them strong or maybe Morgan had told him to. But, again, what did it matter anymore? She had lost John and Molly and Narrow Lane and everything that had mattered to her. Everything that made her feel good about herself and the kind of person she was.

Plus, she had to be more than just lightly buzzed if she was going to deal with Morgan's strange bedroom antics. Who knew what would happen tonight? What crazy shit he would pull.

Back at his hotel room, it nearly seemed like it would be normal sex, for once. Morgan seemed relaxed and happy, kind of surprisingly mellow for him. They spent a long time kissing, which was also kind of surprising for him. He usually went straight for tearing off her clothes, not bothering with the small intimacies like kissing or running a slow hand down the side of her hip.

Zoe lay back on the bed with him kissing her and thought that this was going pretty well. She was definitely buzzed, feeling a little floaty, and Morgan was acting regular. He migrated his kissing down to where her T-shirt met her jeans and unbuttoned them, continuing to kiss her lower abdomen.

She ran her hands through his hair as he wiggled her jeans down lower on her hips, taking her panties halfway down with them. He raised back up to rest on his forearms on either side of her shoulders, his face looking at hers. He ground himself into her with his hips and she raked her hands over his back and gave a little moan.

It felt okay and mostly she wanted to encourage his normal behavior. Maybe the last time they'd been together had been a wake-up call for him and he'd realized he'd gotten out of control and needed to tone it down.

He rolled to the side of her and promptly took off his shirt, pants, and boxers. She reciprocated by pulling her shirt over her head and wiggling completely out of her jeans. She was about to take off her bra when he grabbed her panties and pulled them harshly the rest of the way down her legs. He wadded them into a ball and threw them across the room.

His demeanor had changed.

Shit, Zoe thought. *Shit, shit, shit.*

She braced herself on the bed, waiting for what was next,

and praying the predatory look on Morgan's face just meant he was excited. She decided to try to distract him with a little dirty talk.

"I want you inside me," she said. "Right now. I need it right now."

In a way it was true because if she didn't get him inside her, who knew what would happen next. It was harder to throw her against a wall when he was fucking her. Or at least that's what she hoped.

"You want me?" he said.

"Yeah," she said.

He glared at her. "How badly?"

"Uh, badly?" she said unconvincingly.

His hands were suddenly around her throat, down by her collarbone. She could still breathe but it was terrifying, and not the least bit sexy or thrilling. He put himself inside her, his hands still pressing on her neck.

"Can you let go?" she said. "That doesn't feel good."

He didn't let go. He didn't stop.

Instead he tightened his grip. She felt panicked, her throat constricting perhaps more from fear than from his hold on her. But the fear soon turned to resolve.

Something flipped inside her.

That was it.

She was done with Morgan Cleary.

She was done with letting herself be treated this way.

John was right. Even if they would never be together, even if she had torched their entire friendship, he was right.

She deserved better than this.

"Get off!" she screamed. When Morgan didn't respond right away, she added, "I'm fucking serious, get off me!"

She elbowed him hard just under the ribs and it was enough to make him let go of her neck and roll off her. She had been prepared to follow with a swift knee to the groin if necessary.

She jumped off the bed, coughing, her head spinning. She found her footing and grabbed her clothes, the ones she could locate anyway. She had no idea where her underwear was and didn't care. He could have it as a parting gift. She just wanted out of there.

She tugged on her jeans and was halfway to the door while she was still pulling on her T-shirt.

"Where are you going?" Morgan said, like what had just happened was no big deal.

"You are never touching me ever again," she shouted at him. "I'm done with you. I don't know why it took me this long. You're bat-shit crazy. You think I liked that? You hurting me? You need help. That's all I can say."

She grabbed her purse and rushed out of the room as he called to her saying he was sorry. But this time his apologies didn't matter.

She only stopped to catch her breath once she was in her car. She was breathing so quickly, her heart racing. Tears poured out of her, giant sobs at how she'd let herself be treated. She didn't try to contain them. She let them out, her whole body shaking.

After a time, the tears stopped, like she had emptied herself clean out. She pressed her forehead on the steering wheel and concentrated on breathing for a few moments until everything in her body calmed down. Her pulse slowed and she breathed normally again.

She wiped her face and checked herself out in the rearview mirror. There were no red marks on her neck. Yet. She stared at herself, hard. She thought she'd come to turning points in her life before. Like when she'd decided to turn Étienne in and leave Donnie. But this too felt like a turning point.

She was never going to sleep with just anybody again. She was never going to let someone treat her like Morgan had.

She looked hard at her reflection and made a vow to herself to have self-respect. She had promised as much to John, but promising it to herself felt more substantial.

Chapter 31

ZOE WAS HACKING Trey when she spotted John on Gidget. The first emotion to hit her was jealousy—like seeing your boyfriend with someone new. She was supposed to be riding Gidget.

Her second emotion was happy surprise—she was so glad that John had decided to bring Gidget to Derby Finals after all. Maybe he'd only done it to prove her theory about him being scared to compete against the very best wrong, but still, he had shown up.

The final, and strongest emotion, was regret that things had ended the way they had. Just seeing him from a distance made her ache. Maybe Linda was right—he was the one for her and if she hadn't done so many stupid things maybe he would have come to feel the same way.

She trotted over to him and then came back to a walk. She wasn't sure if he would even talk to her but time had passed—hopefully his anger had faded. It had to, if like Linda said, he asked about her often.

"*Sweetie*, you came!" she said, relying on their old joke to remind him of better times.

He chuckled. "I came."

"That's so great, I mean I'm so happy you're showing her. I would have hated it if she didn't show here."

He gave her horse a once over. Zoe could feel him taking in the perfect tack, the impeccable grooming.

"How's it riding the best hunters in the country? That's Three Wishes, right? Is it as good as you thought it'd be?"

Zoe thought about telling him how it wasn't all that, how it didn't make her anywhere near as happy as it should have.

"It's fine," she said. "But I miss Gidget. I miss everything, actually. Morada Bay, Linda, Dakota, Narrow Lane. How's Molly?"

"She's good," John said.

"That's all you're going to give me about her?"

"What else do you want to know?"

"Have you watched any new movies? Does she have any new favorite songs? How's Sutter? I want to know how everybody is," Zoe said. "I miss you all." It was the closest she would come to saying she missed him.

"We're all fine. Nothing much has changed. Life went on without you, believe it or not."

"I never thought it wouldn't," Zoe said. "That's kind of why I felt okay leaving."

"Yeah, you did feel okay about it."

Zoe blew out a breath. "No, I didn't feel okay." If only John knew how tortured she'd been since leaving and how unhappy she was.

John said, "You know what? It was probably the best thing for me because you were right in a way. I did need a kick in the ass—if I want to make a living I need to play with the big boys. No excuses. So, thank you."

"Um, okay?" she said tentatively. "I mean I'm glad you're here and I know you'll do great. I can't wait to watch Gidget go. Do you have anyone helping you? Depending on where we go in the order I could probably set jumps for you . . ."

"I'm all set," John said.

Having no groom and no one on the ground at a regular show was bad enough, but it was totally inconceivable at a show like Derby Finals.

"You can't be serious," she said.

John gathered up his reins. "You don't have to worry about me anymore, okay?"

"I'm not worried."

"I better get moving."

She called after him, "Say hi to Molly for me, okay?"

"Sure thing."

* * *

There were 77 horses entered in the Classic Round on Friday. Zoe went eighth with Corsica, thirty-second with Milicete, and sixty-eighth with Trey.

Several of the top riders had multiple horses. Then there were riders with only one mount, including a few juniors and amateurs. Zoe knew most of the riders, but there were some from non-horsey areas of the country, like Idaho and Nebraska, without much experience on the national level. Although he was from horsey Bedford, John certainly fit that bill.

The course was beautiful and straightforward—no huge tricks or traps. A nice, welcoming start to the event. There were very few related distances, only one line and two combinations. The first two option jumps came early in the class at fences two and four, verticals with rails covered in roll-top carpet. Then you didn't see another option till jump eight. Jump thirteen, the last obstacle, was the final option.

So a rider could choose to start out over the high options and if their horse started falling apart or the round became shaky they could finish by doing the low options.

Or the opposite—warm up over the low options and go for the high options if the horse was going well by the end. Of course the ideal route was to do all four high options. All three of the horses Zoe was riding were used to doing the high options. Each was a seasoned derby horse. Yes, Trey had won a lot more than the others, but there wasn't a newbie in the group.

Zoe knew everyone was watching her throughout the day. And people at home would be watching the livestream and commenting on posts on Facebook.

This one show felt like it would mean the world for her future. If she rode the horses well and placed in the top ribbons, people would see her as a legitimate contender again.

She'd probably get multiple good job offers for Florida. She'd be even closer to putting her past mistakes behind her.

If she screwed up on such nice horses, they'd write her off as a has-been, as a kid who couldn't make the transition from

junior to pro. They'd no doubt bring up everything again—
the drugs, the saddle stealing. People would probably spread
rumors that she was high or hung-over and that was why
she'd ridden like shit. They'd say they couldn't understand
how it was possible for someone to not do well on a horse
like Trey.

It seemed crazy to wish she could be riding only Gidget—
one unproven horse who had never been to Derby Finals, instead of having three chances on experienced mounts, but the
thought did go through her mind more than once by the time
the class began.

It was like wishing you had one lotto ticket to the Mega
Millions over four tickets to the Daily Jackpot. But she did
wish it. And she had to coach herself to stop those negative
thoughts.

Especially after her first round with Corsica brought a rail
at a slightly tight distance to a jump with lots of fill. Corsica
stalled out a bit, peeking at the fill, jumping up too high, and
snagging the rail behind.

The crowd groaned when it fell.

"Bad luck," Grant said. "Maybe you could have ridden it
a little looser but he still might have had it down."

Zoe hopped off, feeling a pit in her stomach. Grant clearly
wasn't thrilled with how she'd ridden it.

But she had two more to ride and so she had to focus on
those. The groom brought Milicete up.

Milicete was a little bay mare. You wouldn't think she
had a big stride or jump but somehow she did a lot with what
she had to work with. Zoe had to admire her for that. She

tended to be a little on the feisty and hot side so her preparation had included both being lunged and ridden.

Milicete felt nearly tired warming up in the Kentucky heat.

"You'll have more horse in the ring," Grant reminded her as he saw Zoe having to get her going in the schooling area. "Don't let her fool you."

"So she's not so blah she's going to be jumping by braille?" Zoe said.

The mare had rubbed quite a few of the warm-up jumps. Enough actually that the thought occurred to Zoe that maybe Grant had given her something to take the edge off.

While Zoe waited at the in-gate, Cassidy Rancher put in her round on Lawless. Her entourage was lined up along the rail. She rode beautifully and Zoe wondered if Cassidy would have even been a better choice than her to ride Grant's horses.

"Great ride," Zoe told her when she came out of the ring.

"Thanks," Cassidy said. "Good luck!"

Milicete did perk up on the approach to the first fence. Grant was right—she would have more in the ring. Even if he had given her a calming agent, it was clear it wouldn't be enough. The mare's neck and back muscles tightened and her stride quickened. Zoe went into tone-it-down riding mode. Whisper-light leg, no quick moves. Smooth, smooth, smooth.

She managed the course without any big oopses but there was no doubt the mare looked as tense as she felt to Zoe, and the scores in the high seventies reflected just that.

Neither of her first two rides were getting back in the handy round—she was 0-for-2.

Zoe was glad to have John's upcoming round to take her mind off her results so far. She spotted him walking into the warm-up ring and went to go see if he needed help. Even if he claimed he didn't need her help he couldn't very well get ready by himself.

She was approaching the schooling area when she heard Hugo Fine say, "John, what do you usually start over?" and John answer, "Small, square oxer would be great."

She stopped in her tracks. *Good for him*, she thought. *It wasn't all talk—he really was putting himself out there.*

She turned back to the Rolex Stadium, found a seat in the stands, and waited.

When John was at the in-gate, one of Autumn Ridge's grooms wiped off his boots and Gidget's mouth while John and Hugo went over last minute plans.

John picked up a canter and the announcer went over his and Gidget's accomplishments, which were few and paled in comparison to nearly every other rider in the class, even the juniors and the amateurs.

"Now stepping into the Rolex Arena from Bedford, New York, we welcome Girl Next Door. Girl Next Door is an eight year-old Belgian mare by Darco and out of Adelisa II. She placed in the Old Salem Derby, the Lake Placid Derby, and the Genesee Valley Derby this summer with Zoe Tramell handling the riding duties. She also won two derbies at the Vermont Summer Festival. In the saddle today, coming out of our professional divisions, is owner, John Bradstreet. As a junior, he competed in the equitation, winning the CHJA Medal Finals."

John was big on Gidget—not the optimal look. But once she jumped the first jump, Zoe could tell the people watching—and probably the judges too—didn't care much about his size. They were focused on Gidget's jump.

John marched Gidget right around that course, nailing every distance. It was a much better round than Zoe had put in so far that day. And she couldn't have been happier for him. She erupted in clapping and whooping.

It took a few extra moments for the judges to score the round. Surely, they were hesitant to give outrageous scores to a newcomer like John. But when the scores were announced he'd gotten an 86 from the first panel and a 90 from the second panel, plus the high option points.

She made her way to the in-gate to congratulate him but he was surrounded by Hugo's large crew. She tried to maneuver past them and kept waiting for him to look around and see her but he didn't. He was totally absorbed in Hugo's high profile world and who could blame him? It was what she'd told him he needed to do all along.

Zoe turned away, deciding not to bother him.

* * *

Lindsay took a more hands-on role with Trey. Zoe wasn't sure whether that was because Trey was her baby, or because Grant was frustrated with Zoe's riding and needed to step back.

Either way, Grant sat in his golf cart on the side of the warm-up ring and Lindsay stood by the jump on her crutches with a groom who helped her make adjustments.

"He's jumping super," Lindsay said. She was acting very cheerful, like positive reinforcement was her tactic to helping Zoe produce a good round.

As Zoe stood at the in-gate, she rolled her neck from side-to-side, loosening up her muscles. She still felt tight all over.

This was it—her last chance to get through to the handy round. How could she not get through on a horse like Trey?

Was this more pressure than the eq finals? It couldn't be.

The horse before her landed off the horseshoe jump to moderate whoops. Scores in the mid-seventies from both panels flashed up on the board.

Zoe walked into the ring. She took an extra moment to collect herself before she departed into the canter.

Over the first few jumps, she was hyper aware—like she was watching herself ride. When she really nailed a round it was like she didn't even think, like she couldn't hear her own thoughts in her head. Maybe it was like meditating in a way.

But now she was talking to herself in her head about the fact that she was talking to herself—telling herself to settle down and get her head in the game. It was all bad. Very bad.

Only so far somehow she hadn't messed up. Trey was jumping well and she had made it halfway around the course without screwing up. She started bargaining with the horse show gods—promising that if somehow she got around this course without flaw she'd get her shit together.

Finally her mind settled. She felt like she was in one of those movies where people switch bodies, like the mom be-comes the kid and the kid becomes the mom. She was at the part in the movie where the characters go back to their own bodies and can't believe how good it feels.

She was slick and smooth around the rest of the course and she could feel Trey giving good efforts over each jump.

She landed to whoops from Grant and Lindsay. Whoops were their own language. A whoop could mean several different things depending on its tone and duration. It was like a Chinese word in that way—how you said it could alter the meaning completely. There were the money-bought obligatory whoops that trainers had to produce for wealthy clients who managed decent trips. There were the forceful, nearly threatening whoops when a trainer wanted to make sure a judge knew just how goddamn good their kid's round was.

Grant's whoops were surprised, gleeful whoops, like when something good happens to you out of nowhere. They were found money in a jacket pocket.

"Scores are in for Three Wishes. A 92 from panel one and a 94.5 from panel two with all four points for the high options."

When she came out of the ring, Grant said, "Where's that girl been hiding all day?"

Chapter 32

THE HANDY ROUND had a small stonewall trot jump, lots of rollback turns, and a hand-gallop.

A few people blew the trot jump and Jeremy, of all people, had a stop on a roll back turn that he angled too sharply.

Zoe was already on Trey when John went. From a distance, she saw him approaching the trot jump. She closed her own legs on Trey, as if she were on Gidget. She willed John to be patient, to out-think Gidget.

But John used too much leg, anticipating her stopping or sticking off the ground, and Gidget broke into a canter.

When it came time for the hand gallop Zoe figured John might not really go for it. He already had the one mistake at the trot jump and he had told her how he wasn't good at hand gallops. If he really galloped, he could risk having a big flub and embarrassing himself. Probably the smart thing to do was just go a little faster.

But it soon became clear that was not John's intention. Instead of playing it safe, he was figuring he had nothing to lose and was going all out. He kicked Gidget into a real hand gallop and did it just as Zoe had told him to—long before the jump. Zoe held her breath as he approached the jump. She saw the distance he saw, or at least she hoped he saw it. It was a long distance and he needed to keep going. If he doubted himself for a second and stepped off the gas, it wouldn't be pretty.

John kept going and Gidget's stride ate up the ground. The distance they left from was long but bold-long, not desperate-long.

Cassidy came back third to last with Lawless. She laid down a really good trip, putting the pressure squarely on Zoe. She had Cassidy on one side of her and Kendall and Veracity on the other side of her, coming back last.

At the in-gate she realized her shoulders were clenched up practically to her ears and let them drop.

She wanted this so badly. She wanted this win.

Zoe rode like a woman on a mission. She rode like only she knew how to. She was more focused than she'd been all day. Every roll back turn was neat and smooth. Every distance came up perfectly. She waited till she'd made the turn and then effortlessly settled down to the trot and patiently hopped the wall.

She let Trey's stride out for the hand gallop and saw the distance ten strides out. Unlike John's ride, she rode up to the deep one and Trey jumped the moon.

This time Grant's whoops sounded exuberant, not surprised. Her scores were a 92.75 and a 94.25 with all four option points and nine handy points. She had beaten Cassidy but Kendall was still to go.

There was nothing to do but wait and watch. As she watched, Zoe found herself thinking about John's ride more than her own, how he had nailed the hand gallop and what it meant that he had totally and completely put himself out there.

Kendall looked like she barely ever touched the reins. Coming back for the trot jump, it was like all she had to do was think trot and Veracity trotted. He was jumping high and tight with his front end. It was hard not to admire a horse that talented and the partnership Kendall had built with him.

She let him out for the hand gallop and found a more open spot than Zoe had.

Kendall's dad went crazy from the in-gate, hooting and hollering. The crowd stood up and cheered.

The announcer exuberantly issued the scores. "Looks like it's a three-peat for Veracity and Kendall Adams!"

Kendall came out of the ring laying on Veracity's neck, hugging and patting him. Her dad rushed up to clap her on the thigh.

Zoe tried to offer her congratulations too but her voice was lost in all the other people's.

"I hope you're not completely disappointed," Zoe told Grant. "I'm sorry I didn't ride the best all day."

Grant shrugged. "That's horse showing, babe." He didn't say it with any hostility—maybe the second place had dulled the disappointment of the other performances.

The award presentation was chaotic. The horse that was fifth became unsettled and started hopping up and down, nearly rearing.

John had finished tenth, which was a great ribbon. If the

trot jump hadn't snagged him up, he would have been right up there at the top.

She didn't get to talk to him during the presentation. When she came out of the ring, she looked for him. At first she thought he had left, but then she saw him walking toward her.

She slid off and let a groom take Trey from her.

"Your hand-gallop was amazing!" she said. "I feel like I want to say I'm proud of you but I hate when people say they're proud of people. Isn't that something only your parents are supposed to say?"

"Totally," John said. "I wish I hadn't messed up the trot jump. That wouldn't have happened if you were on her."

"You can't be sure about that."

There was so much more Zoe wanted to talk to him about but the PR person for the show interrupted, explaining they needed Zoe at the press conference.

"Go—" John told her. "You're needed."

"We'll catch up later?" Zoe said.

"Definitely."

When all the photos and interviews were over, Zoe went back to the hotel and lay on her bed, still in her boots and breeches. Congratulatory texts rolled in, plenty from numbers she didn't even recognize.

Great ride!

Well done!

You go, girl!

All followed by lots of emojis.

She texted back "thanks" to most of the people and wrote more to people like Hannah and Linda.

By midnight the texts had died down and she still hadn't received any from the one person who really mattered to her.

She decided to write to him, choosing two simple words.

Hey, sweetie.

She stared at her phone, waiting for the three dots to appear that would mean he was typing. Where could he be right now that he wouldn't have his phone? Had he gone out to celebrate with Hugo and his crew? Was he asleep?

Finally, she saw the dots. She clutched her phone inches from her face, waiting.

Yes, darling?

Chapter 33

ZOE AND JOHN STARTED texting every day. At first it was mostly about the horses, Linda, Molly, and Dakota. Then it got more personal. Sometimes it bordered on flirty.

Lindsay started riding without stirrups, gaining back her strength. Zoe knew her time at Lyman Creek would be over soon. She had gotten two calls about possible jobs, one for a big sales operation and one for a trainer that specialized in amateur riders. She wasn't super fired up about either position but they were jobs with decent salaries and nice horses. She could take either position and go to Wellington, and probably find something better over the winter.

When Grant asked to talk to her one day, Zoe was sure it was going to be the thank-you-you've-been-great-we-don't-need-you-anymore speech.

Instead he asked her if she'd be interested in staying on with them through Florida and probably beyond. He said he didn't want Lindsay riding all the babies anymore. He wanted her to concentrate on the more established horses and Zoe would do all the pre-green horses and some of the first years too.

While Zoe would be second to Lindsay and wouldn't be riding in the biggest classes, Grant's horses were top of the line. It was probably better to ride super nice greenies than mediocre experienced ones.

Zoe said she needed a few days to think about it.

But what was there to think about really?

Linda had her sister helping her now and John hadn't even hinted that he might want her to ride for him again.

She told Grant yes the next day.

The following weeks passed with the weather turning so unbearably hot that they had to ride early. Lindsay took her stirrups back and popped over small jumps. They were skipping Harrisburg and Washington, and hoping Lindsay could show by the National.

Kathleen came for a short visit, bringing her son and nanny. She rode a few times as the nanny chased the towheaded boy all over the farm, from the tractor shed to the pond.

When Zoe saw the little boy standing at the edge of the pond throwing sticks in and watching them float, she felt her chest tighten. But the nanny was always right next to him.

Lindsay became friendlier to Zoe, perhaps because she wasn't a threat anymore. She had a bit of a tough exterior but Zoe began to see small moments where Lindsay opened up and let down her guard.

She and Lindsay were at the nail salon on a Monday when Zoe got a text from Linda. It was a photo of her hand . . . with a diamond ring.

She and Eamon were planning a small ceremony at Morada Bay in between the Regionals and the Talent Search Finals. Zoe knew so many horse show marriages ended in divorce. Yet, there was the romantic in her, the one who still hoped for a happily-ever-after movie ending for Linda.

Maybe she and Eamon would be the exception.

She asked Grant for a few days off and found a relatively cheap flight into Newark. One of the best parts of the wedding was Hannah was coming, driving down from Tufts.

And she would see John.

Even though the seats were cramped and the only thing the airline offered for free was a tiny glass of soda, flying felt nearly luxurious since Zoe never really flew anywhere. Usually it was hours in the car.

She tried to remember the last time she'd flown. It was her first year out of ponies when one of Jamie's clients paid for her to fly to Pony Finals to ride a large pony for her.

By the time Zoe arrived at the hotel, Hannah had already checked in. The elevator ride to the fifth floor felt like it took forever. Zoe practically ran down the hallway and was sliding her key card into the slot when Hannah pulled open the door.

Hannah squealed and the two hugged. They didn't let go right away. Finally, when they did, Zoe looked at Hannah to see if anything was different about her. She was still pretty. She still had that somewhat innocent look about her, even though the girl that stood before Zoe now was very different than the girl Zoe had known at Jamie's.

"Oh my God, I can't believe I'm here," Hannah said.

"I can't believe it either."

Zoe hung up the dress she'd brought for the wedding in the closet next to Hannah's. One good thing about working for Grant was that she could actually afford a few things for herself and she was also slowly paying off her credit card debt. Hannah and Zoe laughed because both their dresses were light blue, although Hannah's had a tiered top and Zoe's had a one-shoulder top. Both were just above knee-length.

"Twinsies!" Hannah said.

"I guess blue's in," Zoe said.

They sat across from each other on the beds and talked and talked. Zoe asked Hannah about school and Hannah asked Zoe about working for Grant.

Hannah said, "I'm in a suite, which is basically four rooms that share a common room and a bathroom. I kind of know one of the girls from my chem class and she knew the other two girls, and they're super nice."

Zoe told her, "So I guess I'm going to WEF with Grant and Lindsay. It's pretty good. They have really nice horses and I get to ride a lot. I miss having kids around the barn, though, or other customers. It's just me and Grant and Lindsay."

The subject of John came up when they talked about Linda and the wedding.

"I can't believe I'm finally going to meet him."

"We've been texting a lot since Derby Finals."

Hannah widened her eyes. "Really?"

"He always texts to say good-night."

"Seriously?"

Zoe nodded. "Do you think that means anything?"

"It means you're the last person he's thinking of before he falls asleep. That's huge."

"I don't know. What about you? You can't possibly tell me there aren't tons of cute boys walking around campus?"

Hannah pulled her knees up to her chest and wrapped her arms around them. "I guess there are. I don't know. I still don't feel ready to date yet."

"I doubt Chris is sitting around being celibate."

"Thanks for that," Hannah said, looking away.

"I'm sorry," Zoe replied quickly. "I'm sorry I said that. I don't actually think he got over you fast or anything but I just really feel like you need to live your life and put him behind you. I hate the idea of you not hooking up with guys because of him, or because of one mistake you made and feeling guilty about that."

"It was a pretty bad mistake," Hannah said.

"Still," Zoe said. "Take it from the queen of mistakes . . . life goes on."

Hannah shrugged. "Maybe I'll meet someone, I mean school only just started."

"I hope so," Zoe said.

"I'm considering riding on the school team."

"That sounds great."

"I figure it would be a way to meet more people and I miss the horses."

"You won't find any guys there, though," Zoe pointed out.

"You haven't heard anything about Chris?" Hannah asked. "I mean anything through the grapevine?"

Zoe shook her head. Maybe shaking her head instead of speaking would make it less of a lie because she had heard something. This summer, she'd heard that he'd been seen with a European rider. But rumors always ran rampant about rider hook-ups with Europeans when overseas. It was debatable how much of it was true.

Was it better than his getting back together with Mary Beth? Zoe wasn't sure.

"He's been doing really well," Hannah said. "I'm so happy for him. He was right about being able to ride Athelstane."

"Yeah," Zoe said, glad that they had gotten away from Chris's love life and back to a safer topic—his riding. "Everyone knows he has what it takes to be one of the best. It's all about the horseflesh, though. I heard Delaney isn't too happy with Tommy."

"Really?"

"That's what the rumor is."

"That would have to make Chris feel better about how it ended with Delaney," Hannah said.

That night they went out to dinner with Linda and a few of her closest friends for an unofficial bachelorette party. Dakota came too. She and Hannah hugged and went into the restaurant arm-in-arm, saying how much they had to catch up on. They sat next to each other and Zoe sat across from them, feeling left out. She sensed that Dakota was perhaps acting even chummier with Hannah just to make Zoe feel bad.

The restaurant had a fun and festive vibe, though, and Zoe couldn't stay glum for long, even if Hannah and Dakota talked on and on across from her. Linda looked so happy that her happiness was contagious.

Everyone had margaritas, except Linda and Dakota, of course.

"Some bachelorette party," Linda's sister, Heather, joked.

"Yeah, the bride can't drink and is as big as a house," Linda said.

"You look great," Linda's best friend, Dawn, a trainer from Michigan, said. "You're still totally hot."

Linda laughed. "Oh my God, please."

After the appetizers, Dakota slipped away to go the bathroom and Zoe followed. She found her outside the bathroom, texting.

"Do you have to go?" Zoe said.

"What are you, the bathroom police?"

"No, I just, I wanted to talk to you . . . in private and I wasn't sure when I'd get another chance."

"So you followed me to the bathroom?"

"Yes," Zoe said.

Dakota jutted out her chin. "Well, what is it?"

Man, that girl could be obnoxious when she tried.

"I wanted to say I'm sorry about breaking our pact."

"Who cares?" Dakota said. "That was like ten years ago."

"Well, I care. We promised each other something and I didn't live up to it. I let you down."

Dakota softened a little, her voice quieter and less hostile. "I just wish you'd told me. Like after? I wish you'd come to me and told me you'd had a moment of weakness. I would have totally gotten that. It was that you didn't tell me and I heard it from someone else. I thought we were friends."

"We were. We are! Or I hope we can be again. Next time I sleep with someone horrible you will totally be the first person I call. I just felt so gross about it and I didn't want you to think badly of me."

Zoe swallowed and then decided to come completely clean and confess about hooking up with Morgan the last time in Kentucky.

"See, I'm not mad because you told me this time," Dakota said.

"I realized like right in the middle of it that I was truly done with letting guys treat me like shit. You helped me get to that point, and Linda, and John too."

"He's still hoping you'll come back," Dakota said.

"What?"

"Yeah, totally."

"How do you know?" In all their texts, John had never even hinted about hoping she'd come back.

"Why else do you think he turned down 250K for Gidget?"

"Who offered him *that*?"

"Those people from Illinois. The ones with all the money. Margolis, I think their name is?"

"I never heard that. He never said anything about it."

"Exactly," Dakota said. "He's hoping if he keeps Gidget you might come back and ride her."

"He turned down 250K?" Zoe said, as much to herself as to Dakota.

"I wish you'd come back and work for Linda again. I mean Heather's nice but she's not you."

"Me too, but I want horses to show. More than just Gidget."

"What if I got my parents to buy one for you?"

"That's so sweet," Zoe said. "But you're not asking them to do that. Congrats on getting through Regionals by the way. That was cool."

"Thanks," Dakota said.

When Zoe and Dakota had both returned to the table their main courses were there. A second round of Margaritas was ordered for those who could drink.

After dessert, Linda turned serious. "I can't thank you guys enough for helping me get to this point in my life. For listening to me cry when I dated assholes." Linda looked meaningfully at Heather and Dawn.

"For being there when I found out I was pregnant." Here, she looked at Zoe.

Then she teared up. "I'm just so happy. I'm in love with a great guy and I'm having a baby and I'm getting married!" She wiped at her eyes. "It must be the hormones!"

But everyone was tearing up a little.

If Linda could find love and happiness then maybe someday they all could.

Back at the hotel, Zoe washed up first and was in bed looking at her phone when Hannah came back from the bathroom wearing a cute set of PJs with cows on them. Zoe told her about the offer on Gidget.

"Holy crap," Hannah said. "Wow."

"He needs the money too," Zoe added.

"Did he already text you good-night?"

"Yeah."

Hannah grabbed Zoe's phone and started typing out a message.

"What are you writing? Stop!"

Hannah gave her back the phone. There were five words. *I think I'm falling in . . .*

Zoe shook her head and deleted the text. "Now he probably saw the dots and knows I was writing something and wonders why I erased it."

She typed, *see you tomorrow,* and hit send.

Chapter 34

LINDA WORE A knee-length white dress with an empire waist. She had an understated tiara with a small white veil that Zoe joked she had to wear because it was either that or her sunglasses.

Eamon wore khakis and a blazer. There were no bridesmaids or groomsmen, and only twenty or so people in the folding chairs set up in front of the barn. Eamon's family had decided to postpone a trip until the baby was born. He had a few friends there, mostly other Irish guys from the barn he worked at and Tiernan, the Irish grand prix rider he worked for.

Zoe was acutely aware of John sitting next to her and how nice he'd looked when he'd arrived. She'd subtly elbowed Hannah and it didn't take any more than that for Hannah to realize the man who had just walked in was John.

He had given Zoe a big hug and then said, "You must be Hannah."

"You must be John."

"That's me."

"You're tall. Zoe said you were tall but you're really tall."

"Thanks?" John said, looking from Hannah to Zoe. "That's what sticks out about me most?"

"I guess so," Zoe said. "Maybe it's your best attribute?"

"Ouch." John pretended to act hurt.

"Just kidding. I also said you can ride really well and you pick good horses and you're able to endure watching cheesy movies."

"That sounds like one of those two-truths-and-a-lie things," John said.

Zoe smiled. "But they're all true."

When it was time to be seated, the three of them sat together in the third row.

Hannah leaned over and whispered to Zoe, "You two are so cute together."

Linda's parents walked her down the aisle to where Eamon was waiting, hands folded a little nervously in front of him.

The ceremony itself was sweet and simple. Dakota, in a very pretty boho dress, gave a reading, and one of Eamon's friends sang an Irish folksong.

The only thing that was formal about the ceremony was that they had a minister. Eamon was Presbyterian, not Catholic, Linda had explained, which was lucky because otherwise they would have had to jump through all sorts of hoops to be married in the Catholic Church.

Tears welled up in Zoe's eyes as the minister took them through their vows. She was emotional not because of the words the minister spoke; that was just generic wedding ver-

biage, *to have and to hold, to cherish and to love, etc., etc.* It
was the look on Linda's face, and Eamon's too. But mostly
Linda's. She looked euphoric, but also exceedingly grateful, as
if even though she had hoped for this, she had never actually
imagined it would come true.

Linda deserved the love of a good man and the blessing of
a child on the way more than anyone Zoe could think of. In
Linda, Zoe saw how things you didn't think possible could
happen. How life could surprise you . . . if you let it.

Everyone clapped when the minister told Eamon he could
now kiss the bride and he put one hand behind her head and
pulled her to him, kissing her exuberantly.

They walked down the aisle with everyone standing and
cheering. Horse show people couldn't help themselves from
cheering. Zoe even heard a few whoops.

Eamon and Linda went off to have a few photos taken
and people trickled over to where the caterers were firing up
the grills.

Zoe, Hannah, and John walked over together.

"So what shows are you doing this winter?" Hannah
asked John.

"Did Zoe pay you to ask me that?"

Before Hannah could deny it, he said, "Actually, I haven't
told Zoe this yet but I might go to Gulfport for a few weeks."

"That's cool." Zoe was glad to hear he wouldn't be sitting
home all winter, although Gulfport was a far cry from
Wellington. "Would you bring all the horses?"

"Probably. If I can scrape together the cash. I have my eye
on one more too. I saw one I really like."

"Jumper? Eq horse?" Zoe said.

"I thought he'd be an eq horse but I don't know. I might have another hunter on my hands."

"Really?"

"Well, maybe, we'll see," John said.

Hannah saw Dakota and excused herself to go talk to her. Zoe gave Hannah a quick, annoyed look because she knew Hannah was leaving her on purpose.

"Well, you totally proved you can do the hunter-rider thing at Derby Finals," Zoe told John.

"That might be a bit of an exaggeration," John said. "Let's just say I didn't totally embarrass myself."

"You did really well," Zoe said. "So are you going to keep Gidget and show her?" She was fishing for him to tell her about the offer.

But he said vaguely, "I don't really know yet," and then changed the subject, asking, "What's going on with your job? Are you definitely staying through Florida?"

"It's a good job and they aren't crazy people like most horse show people. If anything, it can be a little boring. I can't believe I'm saying that."

"Boring's probably good for you," John said.

Zoe laughed. "Yeah, no kidding."

"When do you leave for Florida?" John asked.

"Right after The National. The horses go straight from there. We'll go back home and pack up and then meet them there. Any movement on the other horses?"

"You know, a few inquiries. I have them listed on BigEq and they're on my website so I get calls."

"If I can ever help . . . maybe just mention it to a few people. Florida is when everyone's looking."

"Looking to buy something on the show grounds. Not up north."

"Well, maybe when you're in Gulfport. If I had someone seriously interested, they could pay to ship the horse over to WEF for a week or two . . ."

Zoe knew it was a stretch. John was right—if the horse wasn't at WEF, or maybe Ocala, it wasn't going to be high on people's shopping lists.

"I guess I could consider sending a horse to Florida with you. Do you think Grant would go for that?"

"You'd send a horse with me?" Zoe couldn't believe John would trust her that much. "I mean what if I rode it every day in draw reins?"

"Very funny," he said. "And yes, clearly I would trust you."

A small cheer went up behind them from the Irish guys. John and Zoe turned to see Linda and Eamon walking up holding hands. The Irish guys bellowed to Eamon to come have a drink with them and he kissed Linda before joining them.

Linda came over and hugged Zoe. She said she wanted to introduce Zoe to her parents. While she wanted to meet them too, Zoe didn't want to leave John. When she had finally extracted herself from chatting with Linda's parents, Zoe saw that John was busy talking with Heather. Zoe felt a little flash of jealousy, even though she had no reason to think there was anything between them. For one thing, Heather was much older than he was.

For only a few guys, Eamon's friends could make quite a ruckus. The drinks flowed and the voices raised and hearty laughter followed. While there wasn't a dance floor or a DJ, someone set up the barn's Bose connected to an iPhone and soon there was music and dancing.

At first, Zoe and Hannah danced with the Irish guys. Tiernan seemed to gravitate toward Hannah. He was cute with red hair and green eyes. He and Hannah danced together and Zoe thought she detected chemistry between them. He probably knew who she was because of Chris.

Zoe couldn't help but think how Chris would be jealous if he heard Hannah hooked up with Tiernan. Zoe didn't think it would develop into anything more than a hook-up; Tiernan wasn't one for long-term relationships. But it would probably be good for her.

Or would it? The whole point was for her *not* to get involved with another horse person. For her to have her hook-ups at school, outside the gossipy world of the show circuit.

Zoe danced with one of the other Irish guys but she found herself sneaking glances at John. He had gone to get another drink and then was walking back over toward the unofficial dance floor. She saw him look at her and then quickly look away. He was definitely watching her. When the song ended, she walked over to him.

"Not much for dancing?"

"You know, when the occasion merits."

"And this occasion doesn't merit?"

"That makes it sound like I'm not happy for Linda and Eamon. Or like I'm a buzz-kill. I just can't quite get into things. It's a stay-on-the-sidelines kind of night."

"We've all had those kind of nights," Zoe said.

John raised an eyebrow, implying that Zoe hadn't had many.

"I have too," she said.

John looked out over the room. Heather was now dancing with one of Eamon's friends. Hannah was with Tiernan. It wasn't a slow song but they were still dancing close, arms draped around each other.

"I think I'm gonna sneak out, actually," John said.

"You're going home?" Zoe hardly disguised her disappointment. She worried it was because she had danced with the Irish guy.

"Yeah, I'm just going to slip out. I'll see Linda next week anyway. They're only going to New York for two nights on their honeymoon."

She wanted to convince him to stay but what could she say? That Linda would be sad if he left? Linda was having a great time and probably wouldn't notice. The only reason he should stay would be if she told him she wanted him to stay.

"I'll see you around," John said.

Zoe looked back over the wedding crowd. She tried to remind herself of all the good things in her life. She wasn't using drugs. Her life was relatively stable. She had a good job and enough money to pay her bills. She had horses to ride and show in Florida.

So why did it feel so wrong?

Chapter 35

IT TOOK MAYBE forty seconds before she followed John, breaking into a jog. If he drove out before she reached him, it wasn't like she didn't know where he lived, or where to find him. He wasn't getting on a plane to a foreign country and disappearing from her life forever, the final scenes in some of those romantic comedies she'd watched with him and Molly. This wasn't the only chance she'd get to confess to him how she really felt about him.

But if she let this moment go, she was worried she'd never get up the courage again.

The spikes of her heels kept plunging into the grass, slowing her progress. She kept having to stop and grab onto her heel to extract them. Her shoes would no doubt be ruined. But she hardly cared. All she cared about was John.

When she had to bend down and unstick one again she pulled it off instead. Off came the corresponding shoe. She left them in a haphazard pile and ran barefoot toward where the cars were parked.

The grass felt cool and thick on her bare feet. She felt like she was a kid going out to the barn barefoot in the evening to peek in on the horses.

She looked for the back of John's car going down the driveway, thinking he might already be driving away. She was fully prepared to chase him down.

The driveway was empty. Her heart lurched. Was he already gone? Then she looked back at the cars parked on the grass and found him leaning against his car door, his head positioned so it looked like he was staring up at the sky.

What the hell was he doing?

She slowed to a walk, trying to figure it out. Maybe his car wouldn't start? Maybe he had second thoughts about taking off so early?

Or maybe he was having the same thoughts about her that she was having about him. Maybe he too was kicking himself for not telling her how he really felt about her.

He noticed her, perhaps catching a glimpse of her blue dress. He cocked his head—now he was confused.

She spread her arms out to the side in the universal gesture of I'm-not-sure-what-the-hell-I'm-doing-either.

When she reached him, Zoe knew she had to be the one to speak first. "*Sweetie?*"

He smiled. "*Darling?*"

"I like us together. We're good together."

"You mean like as riders, or as people?"

"As people. Aren't we good together?"

"I think we are," John said. "We might even be fucking amazing."

He stepped away from the car and kissed her like he'd

been planning it for a long time, only waiting for the right moment. There was no hesitation, no slow-mo lean-in where you're making sure the other person wants to be kissed before you commit.

So this is what it's like, Zoe thought, as they kissed. This was what it was like to kiss someone whom you felt seriously attracted to but also had a real connection with. It was like bringing two worlds together that had never intersected for her.

But something kept nagging at her. It was that night he'd turned her down.

She pulled away from him. "Wait, why did you turn me down that first time—the night we went out for drinks?"

"I didn't want to be just any guy to you," he said. "I wanted to be *the* guy for you."

* * *

They spent that evening at John's house. Zoe was so happy to see Molly and be back at his house. He put his arm around her at one point and she thought she saw his mother give his father a hopeful look. Clearly Joanne did not know her history or Zoe was certain she would not approve.

Hannah didn't hook up with Tiernan, beyond a few impulsive kisses on the makeshift dance floor. She texted Zoe to find out where she'd gone and they planned to meet up later back at the hotel.

With Hannah sharing her hotel room and John living with his parents, all he and Zoe could do that night was mess around in his car in the far region of the hotel parking lot.

It was the next night, when Hannah had gone back to school, that they slept together.

She worried that after all the wild sex she'd had—most of it by no means good—John might be boring. She'd been with boring guys before and having a guy climb on top of you and basically pump away was okay for a one-night thing but she wanted more with John.

But she shouldn't have worried about any of it, because the moment the door to the hotel room was shut, he was pulling her shirt over her head and leading her to the bed, all the while they were kissing frantically.

He was confident in his actions, but not arrogant, reactive to her responses. It felt good at first and then he changed the angle a little and it didn't feel as good for her and he repositioned himself again.

They got it right and it felt good for both of them and they were both making noise.

"People are going to call downstairs and complain," Zoe said.

"I don't fucking care," John said, between heavy breaths.

He smoothed her hair back around her face and they continued until it was over for both of them.

Zoe couldn't stop smiling as they lay next to each other.

"That was amazing," she said.

"Really? I'm not sure I did anything amazing for you. I mean give me time and maybe I can do amazing things." John made a self-depreciating face. "Or not, I don't know."

"Trust me," she promised. "It was amazing."

Of course it was how they felt about each other, and what he *didn't* do, that made it amazing.

For once Zoe didn't find her head filled with the usual questions like, *will this only be a one-night thing, does he like me, and how can I get him to like me?*

She knew John wanted to spend more nights—and more importantly—days with her.

"Come back east," he said, as if he knew what she was thinking.

"What do you mean?"

"Come ride for me. I'll buy only hunters from now on. You can show them and we can sell them."

"Are you serious?" she asked. No guy had ever offered to change his life for her. Usually she was trying to figure out how to fit into the guy's life.

"Yes, completely."

"The money's not in the hunters. It's in the eq and the jumpers."

"Okay, so we'll do some hunters, and some jumpers and eq."

"But I told Grant I'd go to Florida with them. Can I do that to Grant? Just leave him like I did to you?"

"No, you shouldn't," John said.

"So then what?"

"I think I'm falling in love with you," he said randomly.

"What?" Had any guy ever said he loved her or was falling in love with her? No, not even drunk and in the throes of climaxing. She was totally caught off guard. "How does that answer my question about Grant?"

"It doesn't. Or maybe it does . . ."

She crossed her arms. "Can you stop speaking in riddles?"

"We'll make this work. Maybe you work for Grant through Florida and then come back here in the spring."

Zoe liked his optimism, his faith even though the future felt uncertain and the odds were probably stacked against them.

"What about Morgan and the bad stuff I've done? I mean when I told you about everything that happened in Florida you looked like you were freaked out."

"I was a little freaked out but that was before I got to know you. Shit happens. Shit happens that you didn't really want to happen or plan for it to happen. I think I'm okay with letting your past be in the past."

"Okay," she said, still a little tentatively.

"Okay—what are you saying okay to?"

"Okay to making it work."

"What about the part where I said the love thing—not sure I should repeat that. Too much, too soon, too crazy?"

There was so much she'd done in her life that had been too much, too soon, too crazy but John was the first guy she'd been with that made her feel good about herself and the person she could be. Wasn't that what finding the right person could do—make you your best self?

"I think I'm falling in love with you too," she said.

About the Author

KIM ABLON WHITNEY lives with her husband and three children in Newton, Massachusetts. In addition to writing fiction, she is a USEF 'R' judge in hunters, equitation, and jumpers and has officiated at the Washington International Horse Show Junior Equitation Finals, the Capital Challenge, the Winter Equestrian Festival, Lake Placid, and the Vermont Summer Festival. She also runs the blog Below the Cutoff: A Look at the Horse Show Life. Keep in touch with Kim on Facebook, Twitter, Instagram, and at:

www.kimablonwhitney.com

CPSIA information can be obtained
at www.ICGtesting.com
Printed in the USA
FSHW012004190821
84192FS